Student Conservation Association Crew and leader Jeanne Anderson after crossing the Mckinley River Bar, Denali National Park. August, 1992.

WALKING ON TREES

VIEWS FROM THE BACK COUNTRY

by

Russell Hanbey

Walking on Trees: Views From the Back Country
© 2014 by Russell Hanbey

Interior photographs
© 2014 Russell Hanbey, unless otherwise noted.

Front cover photograph "Kennedy Hot Springs cabin with Whitechuck River in foreground, Glacier Peak Wilderness, July 1975" ©
2014 Bernie Smith

Back cover photograph (top) "The author crossing the Fire Creek
Bridge, Whitechuck River Trail, Glacier Peak Wilderness, July,
1975" © 2014 Bernie Smith

Back cover photograph (bottom) "Student Conservation Association
crew and leader Jeanne Anderson after crossing the Mckinley River
Bar, Denali National Park, August, 1992" © 2014 Russell Hanbey

Book and Cover design: Vladimir Verano, Third Place Press

Author contact: www.russhanbey.com

ISBN: 978-0-9914940-0-2

This book is dedicated to the creators and maintainers of America's Wilderness Preservation System, now 50 years old.

Contents

OTHER BACKDROPS

ARTICLES

Ongoing generations of climbers, researchers and high elevation
explorers have bivouacked at Camp Muir on the upper slopes of
Mt. Rainier. This sketch details a long and exhilarating day on the
mountain for Carroll Vogel and his Sahale Construction team as
they bring their craftsmanship to the reconstruction of this iconic
settlement.

Crowder and Tabor, in their now-rare book *Routes and Rocks*, line
out a classic off-trail scramble in the North Central Cascades. Step
outside the lines on the Black Mountain High Route and walk
along as this escapade unfolds step by vertiginous step.

This article depicts the character-rich history of the Kennedy Hot
Springs area and what remains of what nature put asunder after a
series of devastating floods.

Visiting marmot on Green Mountain Lookout, with Dome Peak in background, North Central Cascades. July, 1990

INTRODUCTION

THE EXTERIOR LANDSCAPES OF THE NORTHWEST are full of stories, many of them untold. This compilation pays tribute to these astounding natural resources as seen from high ridgelines, lake basins, deep watersheds, wilderness tracks, trail corridors, and back country roads. Most of the stories and articles are told from the perspective of a U.S. Forest Service seasonal worker learning the business and plying his trade over 14 summers. In contrast, several accounts describe experiences in natural settings beyond the Cascade Mountains. There is humor and some darkness in these stories, yet all echo the influence of a life spent in or near wild places.

For long time walkers, the stories and articles may be evocative of past trips into the Cascade Mountains. New hikers will get teasers about places to visit in addition to historical overviews of several popular hiking locations in the region.

Settings for the stories range from Mount Rainier to Mount Baker with visits to Mount Pilchuck, Glacier Peak, White Horse Mountain, Green Mountain and Black Mountain in between. The broader view spreads out to the Dingle Peninsula in Ireland and Denali National Park in Alaska.

Also included are previously published articles, including a selection about the Black Mountain High Route reprised from a 1976 edition of *Signpost Magazine*. Another entry, "20 Loads," appeared in

2008 in *Washington Trails Magazine* and the last, "Wanderer's Wayside," was featured in an issue of the *Seattle Times Pacific Magazine* in 2009.

The collection is not intended to be a hiking guide. These accounts were written over a number of years and local conditions have changed over time. For example, access to the Kennedy Hot Springs area has reverted back to where it was over 100 years ago and the Green Mountain road and trail are unmaintained as of this printing. Regardless, it is hoped that *Walking on Trees* may give the reader a chance to savor what they've already experienced, get a bead on somewhere new to explore, or just enjoy one person's written response to the value and beauty of remote landscapes.

With one exception, all of these events and observations reflect true events. Some names have been changed to protect identities. In the end, this is my honest effort to take the reader on a side by side walk out past the end of the road

PROLOGUE

UP A NORTHWEST TRAIL

THREE HOURS OF HIKING UP A ROUGH TRAIL leave me high on a ridge that could be almost anywhere in the Cascade Mountains of Washington. I catch my breath, lift my head and try to embrace the vast depth of my surroundings. I'd seen similar vistas many times before but was still moved by what was before me. At eye level, there were ridgelines near and far. Higher up were notched sets of rough peaks, each one competing for the same space like large teeth in a small mouth. Underpinning each high point were snowfields, gullies, and rocky features in numerous shapes and configurations.

Two hours earlier, I'd pulled into the trailhead keen for a walk in the woods. I hadn't even laced up my boots when I caught the fragrant and evocative odor of the riverside cottonwoods, always an indicator of early summer in the Cascades. Overhanging trees and moss guarded my first eager strides through a wet tunnel of chest-high leafy plants. Off in the distance came the sound of a Varied Thrush, easily one of the most inviting and reassuring bird songs in these mountains.

As I moved through the lower stretches of trail, most of my footfalls found soft landings on a matted surface of old hemlock needles and rotted leaves. As I turned the corner on the first of many switchbacks, the grade of the trail started to rise. The understory plants thinned out and I was surrounded by the remnants of 50-year-old logging operations. Rotted stumps with springboard incisions around their edges were everywhere; a sure sign of old growth forests giving

1

way to timber cutters with sharp tools and strong backs. Surrounding these artifacts were stands of maturing second growth Douglas firs, Western hemlocks, and an occasional red cedar of tremendous girth that had dodged the crosscut.

After another half hour, the increasingly rocky path climbed and found its way over small streams and outcrops. The over story pulled back and the trail corridor opened up with low clouds disguised as mist adding a mystical element to the ascent. Driblets of water gathered on trailside plants wetting my boots and lower legs. I was now in the Silver fir zone with its companion plants of Cascade Azalea, Alaska huckleberry and Mountain ash.

The pathway continued ever upward as it left the wooded complex of spurs and draws into longer traverses of subalpine parkland. Tree clumps featuring Mountain hemlock and Alaska cedar added contrast to what was now a complex of avalanche chutes and vast meadows. Early season flower shoots arched toward the sun would come later. An occasional peeping bird would divert my eye. Even in the chill of the morning, sweat trickled down my back. This was most noticeable at water breaks after I'd dropped my pack and cold air touched the sodden back of my shirt.

I leaned into the climb and thought about the many times I'd walked up steep trails with a heavy load. There were some pathways I'd been on numerous times and they never magically flattened out. I constantly felt the tug of gravity pulling me backward as I went up. Yet, here I was, trudging upward eager to see what was around the next corner.

The repetition of effort brought my legs to a certain achy point but got no worse. The trail seemed to wrap around itself as it ascended up a narrow gulley, all the while stitched together by switchbacks and climbing turns. You could step forward with a certain confidence that you were both advancing and moving upward. Yet at the same time, you were on a static path that remained laced to the landscape.

The physics of ascending the trail seemed more complex than it really was. Intuitively, I knew where to place my feet so I wouldn't slip or dislodge a loose rock. There was an unthinking momentum as

I leaned forward into the next footstep while my level of awareness remained high. An innate sense of balance kept things on track.

The trail eventually leveled off and found its way onto the ridge-line. The downward tug and pull inherent in the steep grade below eased off as each new step found its way onto mostly level ground. This was a thrilling moment on the hike when the exertion of the climb transitioned into a measured stretch of effortless walking. Views often dominate these moments but lines of sight also stop at the nearest curtain of foliage. No matter, these unique sections of trail reenergize and support the notion that the trudge to the top had been worth it. In the Cascades, many such spots are etched in my memory. The Pacific Crest Trail near the upper Kennedy Creek crossing east of Darrington is one such memorable segment.

Eight miles of climbing, twisting trail above the Whitechuck River leads to a sweet section of horizontal hillside walking. Further south, four miles of relentless uphill clambering on the Lost Creek Trail leads to a long and level walk through meadows as the trail winds its way eastward towards Sunup Lake and Lake Byrne. In addition, it's hard not to enjoy the high moraine walking along the Scott Paul Trail on Mount Baker or the ridge top walk from the upper end of the Boulder Creek Trail to Juanita Lake and Purple Pass above Lake Chelan.

Once the ridge is won, the trail often leads to some kind of pass or high point. For me, this is sometimes the end of the trail and the turnaround point. Lunch is eaten, boots removed, and a sweaty tee shirt is laid out to dry.

Other times, I will continue onward and downward at a sharp angle as the trail descends into the next drainage. As it drops over the edge, the terrain is frequently pinched down and the trail has to find its way back to tree line at an angle that can be touchy. If it's a north-facing slope in the Cascades, then it can lead to a sharp descent over steep snow. Here, an ice axe comes in handy as a safety tool and third arm. Once down a ways, the trail often bottoms out in a pile of avalanche debris. Somewhere nearby, the established trail reemerges and continues on.

The trail can also lead to a fire lookout or viewpoint. This means that the trail can get steeper and more exposed. Proper route finding becomes acute with the presence of late snow. I can either follow someone else's boot prints and exercise blind faith that they know the way or strike out on my own. Either way, there is usually something rewarding at the end.

At the crest of a ridge is also where I've found curious way trails. These informal foot paths can be taken to a nearby lake, hidden campsite, toileting spot, dead end, vista, or a spot for a high mountain tryst. The end result might also be a head scratching mystery as to why the trail headed off in this direction in the first place. All in all, high points in the Cascades are busy places. Weather breaks occur there, animals show themselves, and hikers converge. It's both open and enveloping.

After an hour of gazing, I begin the descent. The boot laces are tightened and the hip belt hitched up. Long trips back down trails provide a lot of time for introspection. It can be quite meditative where the brain doesn't process much beyond the next step. Or the descent can involve deeper thoughts with a reliance on muscle memory to keep from stumbling forward. Either way, a new set of muscles will eventually begin to complain with the knees as aching companions. The trailhead is soon earned and the ridgeline as a focus for the day morphs into a memory.

The author crossing the Fire Creek Bridge, Whitechuck River Trail, Glacier Peak Wilderness. July, 1975 Photo by Bernie Smith

Howard Barstow, Darrington Ranger District Fire Control Officer,
on the final steps to Miners Ridge Lookout, Glacier Peak Wilderness
Photo courtesy of Darrington Ranger District, U.S.F.S.

SEASONS in the FIELD,
MOUNTAIN SITTING,
and OTHER EXPLOITS

Early Up On Whitehorse

THE PEAK-A-BOO VIEW OF MOUNT THREE FINGERS offered itself up as expected. The clouds had lifted and I was once again reassured by the surprising vista of this remarkable mountain on the southeast horizon. It was the middle of June and I was ten miles along Highway 530 headed east into the Cascade Mountains. This trip would turn out to be as poignant as my first up this rural road 47 years before.

Getting to this point from Seattle involved a mind-numbing jaunt north up Interstate 5. Over the years, the landscape along the freeway corridor had filled in with suburban sprawl, casinos, strip malls, and the usual frontage road congestion. At the Darrington turn-off, though, the backdrop shifts. Farm fields appear as the highway narrows down from four lanes to two. Just past Arlington, the road is obligated to share the valley bottom with the North Fork of the Stillaguamish River. This steelhead rich river meanders from one side of the valley to the other, with the road bisecting the broad sweeps of its trajectory towards Puget Sound. The road isn't the only manmade construct heading inland. An old railroad right-of-way peeks out occasionally from under its cloak of red alders and blackberries to give a hint of days gone by.

For me, the trip up valley to Darrington is evocative and never disappointing. The vertical relief on both sides of the valley increases in size and scale as the ridgeline builds from soft foothills to steep escarpments in less than 20 miles. The over-logged bumps outside of

Arlington give way to 7,000-foot mountains with north facing slopes that never lose their snow. Water cascades down to the Stillaguamish on feeder streams with names like French, Deer and Seaglesen. The hamlets of Oso and Trafton come and go in a blink. There are tree farms, saw shops, subsistence ranches, vacation cabins, small nurseries, and a scattering of homes. In the end, the peaks lord over everything and dominate the landscape. The bulk of Mount Higgins, Three Fingers, and Jumbo Mountain capture the foreground on the way up followed by distant views of Mount Pugh, Whitechuck, and finally Glacier Peak.

The most sublime spot for me is two miles east of Swede Heaven, the name place for a settlement five miles before Darrington. The road opens up from a corridor of tall second growth firs and hemlocks into a tract of cleared land and meadows. Here is where I get to pull over onto Engles Road (named after Forest Service Ranger Harold Engles and his wife Anna Mae) and enjoy the full frontal view of the mass of Whitehorse Mountain.

Facing south, my eye moves upward from soft, flat pastures, to a layer of evergreens. From there, rough lower slopes reveal a maze of spurs, draws, snow and ice which ultimately lead to an exposed rock summit of 6,852 feet. Whitehorse is a lot of vertical scenery to absorb in one gulp but it defines and dominates the adjacent landscape.

A bit further up the road are the rodeo grounds, a cemetery, some small businesses and finally the town of Darrington. Darrington is a working town. No pretense, no fluff, just the foundation for a hardscrabble existence for many. Just past Mr. Ed's Burger Barn, I pull into the ranger station and the memories flood in once again. It could have been 1967.

It was then that I showed up as a shave tail 19-year-old looking to make my mark. Before that, I had floundered about looking for decent summer work that mostly didn't exist. I was a baby boomer and we were the "pig in the python" generation competing for everything including the few job openings scattered about the Northwest for seasonal workers. Just after my sophomore year in college, a friend of a friend finally helped me nail down a rare opening with the Darrington

Ranger District as a fire lookout. I had no idea what I was getting into but grabbed the job without hesitation.

Along with the other seasonal employees for the Forest Service, I showed up in the middle of June for orientation and work. We were all full of apprehension and eagerness. I had accepted my impending job as a fire lookout without much forethought; just blind hope that it would all work out. My expectation was that things would move pretty slowly until the actual day arrived when I would head out to begin my assignment. I didn't know that my first day on the job might also be my last.

The day before, I'd made my maiden voyage up the valley, found the Ranger Station, checked in, and was directed to find a place in the main bunkhouse. I settled into a corner bunk and stowed away my belongings. I can still remember how stale and dusty the mattresses were. Another summer hire who looked as green as I was moved in and we spent the rest of the day cleaning up the place and piecing together some kitchen, dining room and living room furniture we found in an old barn on the compound. By 11:00 p.m. that first night, I was bushed and headed for my bunk. I tossed about in the darkness, partly because of my wonderment about what was in store for me and partly because the mattress was lumpy and smelled like old socks.

I got up early the next day and headed over to the fire warehouse where I had been told to report. It was hard to ignore the early morning smell of creosote, a coal tar preservative used to coat the piles of lumber stacked around the compound. Nearby, four guys around my age were gathered to await their fate, just like me. They were smoking and joking nervously.

Before long, the Fire Control Officer, Howard Barstow, ambled up with a bemused look on his face. I had talked to him briefly in the office the day before and he seemed to be a pretty important figure at the station. As he stood before the group, I noticed his emerging potbelly, working man's tan and lump of chew behind his lip. Here was a man who had spent much of his life immersed in the mountains and watersheds that defined this countryside.

"Good morning. You boys up for a little hike?" Howard said.

We all looked at each other with some surprise. We thought we'd be working around the station or getting our gear together but didn't expect to go on a hike.

Howard grinned and told us that a lightning storm had come through a couple of days earlier. A fire crew had headed up to douse a small fire on Whitehorse Mountain. They'd left a few things behind that we may as well hike up and retrieve. It didn't seem like a big deal. Little did anyone know that one person would quit that day and the rest of us would be tempted to do the same.

Howard wandered off telling us to, "grab a lunch and some rain gear and meet at the crummy in ten minutes." I didn't know what a crummy was but it didn't sound promising.

I scrambled around for a sandwich and my cheap plastic raincoat. Soon we were heading out of town in a beat up passenger van and towards the base of Whitehorse Mountain, about ten miles away. In the back of the rig were a half dozen empty fire packs and some tools. Howard hadn't come along, mumbling something about needing to test someone for a Federal Driver's License later that day.

He'd sent his assistant, Dennis "Whitey" White, who had less to say than Howard. He just chuckled a lot and answered "yep" or "nope" to most questions. He was built like a fireplug and wore a brimless red felt hat. His hands were textured and gnarled from having made a living in rough conditions for many years. As it turned out, Whitey was a professional forester from Maine who'd migrated out west to test his mettle in the woods of the Northwest.

We turned off the main highway and bounced along an old mining road for about four miles until we pulled up to a log blocking the road.

"Okay, cowboys, throw your gear in those empty packs and let's head out," Whitey said.

Everyone grabbed a pack, noticing immediately that it was nothing more than fabric stretched across a metal frame with two thin strips of flat cord for shoulder straps. We looked at each other nervously as we searched for this so-called trail we were going to hike.

None was in sight. Instead, we crawled over the log and headed further up the road until it disappeared into a thicket of brush. In the distance, I could hear the heavy rumble of water slicing down from the face of the mountain directly above us. We couldn't see the mountain because we had just pushed our way into the same thicket that had blocked our path earlier. I immediately stumbled on a hidden log and fell flat on my face.

Trying to compose myself, I pressed on with the others slipping down a muddy bank only to face a narrow, frothing stream cascading rapidly down from hidden snowfields above us. Any misstep and we'd get soaked. Whitey didn't even break his stride as he boulder-hopped across the stream and into the brush on the other side. We looked at each other, waiting for someone to take the first step. What was the hidden information that had allowed Whitey to cross with such ease?

There were rocks to land on but they were submerged and slippery. One of the other recruits decided to give it a try with a hand on an overhanging branch to get started. His strategy for crossing was to splash across as fast as he could and hope for the best. It was devoid of Whitey's finesse and technique but it worked. The rest of us followed suit. Ten minutes on the trail and I already had a bruised ego and wet feet.

We rushed to catch up with Whitey as if we had passed some kind of test. I didn't even look up—I just kept pushing up the faint trail toward someplace unknown. We began gasping for air as the route got steeper. It was slightly warm and very humid in amongst the alders we were battling. Slide alders are constructed by nature to grow in packed mats in a downward fashion. This allows them to bend and fold with the snow load and tolerate the avalanche chutes where they thrive. They are also not constructed for human beings to climb through unless, of course, you're a veteran bushwhacker like Whitey who barely stopped to push a branch aside.

After another half hour, I felt my feet slipping on something. I looked down and noticed I was walking on snow. How could this be? It was the middle of June. Regardless, the snow was heavy and compacted in such a way that is was difficult to get secure footing.

Naturally, Whitey didn't slow, but instead took a sharp turn to the right and back out towards the stream we had crossed earlier. We tagged along and found ourselves traversing an increasingly steep snowfield. Whitey took the lead up a gully that threaded its way down steeply from the now exposed snowfields up above. I could hear water rushing underneath the snow as I tiptoed along. What I thought were branches sticking out of the snow turned out to be the tops of evergreen trees. I was walking on trees!

Once again, the group was thrown into a predicament as Whitey disappeared into a jumble of trees on the other side. This time we had to work our way 50 feet across a sharply angled snowfield that was not only icy but opened up into a gaping hole below. No one was prepared for this. I was beginning to think this was a setup.

Someone else took the lead and somehow made it across without slipping. I followed along with my stomach in my throat. I had very little tread on my new J.C. Penney work boots but was able to kick away at the hardened snow and produce sketchy but secure footing. I made a point of not looking down or listening to the roar of the stream in the pit below me. It worked and I was across before I knew it. Relieved, I joined in to cheer on those still pondering their fate on the other side. Most followed suit, except one of the other new guys who took one step and slipped down three feet. He turned around and headed back down for the crummy and the end of his Forest Service career.

Whitey led us on up onto a spur where lightning had struck several days before and burned about an acre of duff and small trees. It was no big deal by Forest Service standards but enough to merit an all-out suppression effort. In this case, it required the extensive use of hoses and a pump on top of the basic shovel and axe approach to fire fighting. Our job that day was to pack up and remove all of the hoses that had been left by the fire crew.

Whitey paired us off and directed us to follow out different lines of hose. He showed us how he wanted the hoses rolled and secured and sent us on our way. The terrain was steep and the hoses tangled. My partner and I began pulling in a 300-foot line of connected hose up and over a sharp buttress. The hose was covered in soot and mud and resistant to rolling into a bundle. There was no flat ground on which to work with any ease. After several false starts, we discovered that we could gather and align the hose into decent 50-foot bundles and bring them down to a place Whitey called the bone yard. This was an open area where chunks of smoldering wood were brought to burn out and die during a wild fire. It was also a gathering place, a spot where everything was mustered for distribution or storage.

We wrapped six sections of hose and delivered them to the ever-growing pile. We repeated the process several times until it was time for lunch. It was the only time I saw Whitey do anything resembling rest all day. His pace was slow, steady and continual. He didn't take breaks; he just slowed down for a minute. Here was a man at ease with his body and his abilities. Nothing in this environment seemed to intimidate him.

I, on the other hand, was sweaty, tired, covered with soot, and keenly aware of everything around me. This first real break of the day offered me the chance to look out over the valley and savor our bird's eye view. The pungent smell of subalpine fir and Alaska cedar, the rush of water, the haunting melody of thrushes and the sight of my first mountain hummingbird carved some deep notches in my soul that day.

I also discovered that the adrenaline rushes from earlier in the day were mixing with the residue of accelerated physical effort and that I was measuring up to this challenge that Howard had orchestrated. Later on, I would see the benefit of testing new mountain workers so that they would know what to expect and what the Forest Service could expect of them. Today, we'd all sink or swim. I knew I could swim, at least in this water, and was reassured.

The trip down, loaded with rolls of hose, felt different than the trip up. Most of us didn't hesitate on the snow finger or at the stream crossings. We kept up with Whitey.

We cruised back through Darrington towards the ranger station with a certain amount of grimy pride. I glanced out the window as we bounced along. Not only were these mountains painting a backdrop for my first experiences that summer but so too the logging settlement of Darrington. Here was a little town with a big reputation.

Everyone in this settlement was known to lead a vigorous life and not hold back when it came to hard work, strong opinions, and humor. The place also was regarded as an intolerant, closed community by its urban neighbors down valley. I eventually discovered that was nonsense. What really defined Darrington were strong family connections, pride in a spirited existence and a working, albeit controversial, relationship with the natural resources nearby.

There was a community-wide level of trust with which I was unfamiliar. Before long, I was able to open an account at the local grocery store. I could order, from afar, the supplies I needed delivered to Green Mountain, where I was serving as the fire lookout for that summer. No one questioned my credit or credibility.

While in town, many of us would troop down to the Red Top Restaurant in the morning for breakfast. The matronly waitresses would fix us a take out lunch for the day. We were able to put our expenses on a tab, payable when we got paid. Even though there was a natural tension between the loggers and the Forest Service, none of us new guys felt any of it as we ate elbow to elbow with the local work force.

"Hello fellers, how was your day on the mountain?" Howard greeted us as we pulled into station.

"Looks like you found some hose."

It was my nature to try and come up with wisecracks, but I was bushed and ready for the day to end. I didn't have much to say, nor did my co-workers as we unloaded the crummy.

"Seems to me these young men are a little ripe and need to get near a hose with water in it," Whitey said to Howard.

"Yep, I've got one hooked up over there by those trucks," Howard replied.

Lined up in a side parking lot were a dozen Forest Service rigs. They all needed washing. We were already dirty so maybe this wasn't going to be so bad. What we didn't figure on was the need for a putty knife.

As it turned out, on hot days the gentleman tobacco chewers at the Ranger Station would travel about spitting their loads of snoose out open windows. Not all of it cleared the side of the rigs, so it splattered the side panels and dried as they drove. This is where the putty knife came in and the finale of our first day.

After that initiation, I dove in head first not knowing if I'd come out the other end intact. For many of us, seasonal work in wild areas was akin to a rite of passage into adulthood. For starters, the work was usually far from home. This meant traveling alone or with a buddy to some remote locale. Once there, we had to figure out the culture of the Forest Service, the local Ranger District and the town where we were going to live and work. At the same time, we needed to set up shop and figure out where to buy necessities, clean clothes, fix an injury, party on Saturday nights, and take care of all the day-by-day stuff usually done on familiar ground. The same could be said, of course, about going off to college or into the service, but striking out for a Ranger District on the backside of a mountain somewhere left the world of the convenient and predictable behind for one of the unknown and scarcity. This was a part of the allure and added fodder to our idealistic notions of the experience.

Doing well the first year could lead to many subsequent seasons, most often in the same place if the work was available. The first assignment was like a first love, and a sense of loyalty evolved. For me, faces became familiar; I started learning the landscape and my skills started to gel. I attained some seniority, which allowed for better or different jobs the next summer, and first dibs on the best beds in the bunkhouse. Trust was built to the point that many of us at an early age were embracing leadership and higher levels of responsibility. One season you rode in the crummy, the next season you drove it. One year you worked with a professional, the next you were on your own. All of this elevated our confidence and a feeling of what we're supposed to do when we grew up. This was the foundation I built as I took on a variety of jobs that would stretch out to many more summers over the years.

None of this was lost on me as I pulled into the back lot of the Ranger Station 47 years later. The view up through the even taller Douglas firs and hemlocks towards Whitehorse Mountain hadn't changed nor had the nervous excitement of a group of fresh-faced young men and women waiting by the fire warehouse for their summer to unfold.

Green Mountain Summer

JOURNEYING BY FOOT ON THE UPPER SLOPES of Green Mountain in the North Central Cascades is a mountain walker's utopia. The classic forested walk up the south facing slope on the lower mountain gives way to subalpine parklands and verdant herbaceous meadows. On a clear day, views are of such a depth that it's easy to stumble on the trail while gazing, stupefied, in all directions.

After 3,000 feet of climbing up four miles of trail, the summit is achieved along with a 360-degree overview of peaks and valleys too numerous to absorb in one panting glance. The panorama is that of multiple shades of green intermingled with geologic ribs and sills that reach out in every direction. Ridge after ridge of vertical relief is capped by rocky outcrops and snowy fingers of white as the interior of the North Central Cascades reveals itself. Hovering to the southeast is Glacier Peak, historically known as DaKobed or the "Great Parent" for the tribes in the region. Defining other parts of the horizon are serious mountains with the names Snowking, Buckindy, Eldorado, and Sloan.

The summit's unobstructed view over valley bottoms, heavily forested slopes, and emergent ridgelines prompted the U. S. Forest Service, caretakers of this landscape, to begin using Green Mountain as a fire lookout in 1926. The peak itself is actually a diminutive member of a larger massif of mountains that define the North Central Cascades. As a junior member of this collective, the summit of Green Mountain looks up, around, and through the legs of the whole circular show. If a lightning storm pushes through then Green Mountain Lookout has a front row seat to see lightning strikes and eventual smokes. If errant loggers or campers trip off a lowland fire, then observers on Green Mountain are positioned to spread the word to Darrington Ranger District fire personnel.

Green Mountain was one of 20 lookouts that once crowned various peaks in the Darrington area, each with its own personality and assets. High points such as Glacier Ridge, Mount Pugh, Circle Peak, Barlow Point, Huckleberry Mountain, Mount Higgins and even the barn at the ranger station provided skyline views in all directions. During World War II several remote lookouts, including the dramatically exposed Mount Three Fingers, were staffed during the winter as Aircraft Warning sites.

After the war, the advent of aerial reconnaissance and infrared sensing of fires reduced the need for human eyes, leading to the demise of most of these facilities. By 2000, the only remaining lookout buildings were Miners Ridge, Mount Three Fingers, Mount Pilchuck, and what's left of North Mountain. Miners Ridge, once described as the "Shangri-La of Fire Lookouts" by fire lookout historian Ray Kresek, is the only lookout still staffed in the summer by a volunteer.

Of the 656 original lookouts built in Washington State, 107 are still standing and 30 are still in service. All of these lookouts were nothing more or less than the people who worked in them over the decades. People who serve as fire lookouts are strongly independent and sometimes eccentric people, so it's no surprise that a cult of personalities surrounds most lookout lore. Note this quote from Dick 'Lightbulb' Winders, former Green Mountain Lookout: "Green Mountain was like a wife to me. It was a goddess. It was the thing I loved most in the world. How can you turn your back on something like that?"

When fire lookouts began manning Green Mountain in 1926, there was no building. The first sentinel, Hubert Wilson, lived in a tent below and hiked to the lookout daily with his compass to spot fires. In 1928, an emergency ground wire was strung from near the summit to the Suiattle Ranger Station 5,500 feet below. The next summer, John E. Schwartz moved into an 8'x10' wall tent on an adjoining ridge and used a small fire finder affixed to a rock on the summit. He stated in a later interview that, "There was no shelter here and since I had no material with which to construct even a temporary one. It was necessary to spend long hours each day sitting on a rock in the sun."

The building that was eventually constructed in 1933 was a standard Alladin L-4, hipped roof 14'x14' Lookout House. It was the oldest lookout of its type in the Mt. Baker/Snoqualmie National Forest when it achieved National Register of Historic Places status in 1990. Who built the structure itself is unsubstantiated, but most likely the 45 Civilian Conservation Corps workers stationed in the river valley below were involved in the construction. Lookout buildings were often produced as kits, disassembled, and rebuilt onsite. The pre-built materials for Green Mountain were packed up a trail beginning near Downey Creek. The loads were fashioned to accommodate mules carrying lumber no longer than seven feet long. This was the upper limit a mule could manage on the running switchback turns common to western trails built at the time.

In 1967, I was next in a long line of lookouts that would find their way to the old building and continue the legacy. Before that happened, there was some ground work to do. Howard Barstow, the Fire Control Officer, took three of us to North Mountain Lookout for an orientation to our jobs. This was a new lookout built on a 40 foot tower, just seven miles by road outside of town.

We went up on a beautiful day. I was staggered by the bird's eye view and the unique world of forest fire lookouts. Our introduction to our impending assignments as fire watches included fire spotting, radio usage, weather reading, map reading, taking care of the lookout and ourselves. Howard filled us in.

"What you want to do is make a sweep of the territory every hour of the day, learn the lay of the land, know where the campgrounds are, what logging operations are active, and where people gather. Get to know the weather, especially the difference between a cloud and a column of smoke. And, of course, there's always lighting. We don't get a lot of hot clouds coming through here, but when they do, it's a real show. See that little stool over there with the glass insulators on the legs. That's to stand on when a lightning storm goes overhead."

I gulped.

"Don't worry, we haven't lost anybody yet. This stool is your best friend. You'll need it using the fire finder, which is made of metal, during a lightning bust. The Osborne Fire Finder is your key to good fire location. It's centered here in the middle of the lookout and allows you to take a reading on fires that are both above and below the lookout. The base of the fire finder is a topographic map with the lookout in the very center. You look through this sliding peephole and line up the fire with the crosshairs on the other side to tell the fire's direction. The metal tape across the middle lets you estimate how far away it is."

Howard was on a roll.

"After you pick up a smoke and document it with the fire finder, you fill out this Fire Report and call it into the office. Pretty simple, huh?"

We looked at each other with some trepidation. This was a little more technical than I had counted on. But, with a couple hours of practice, we all caught on and began to appreciate the genius of the tool.

"Anybody for a chew before we head on down?"

Howard was probably kidding, but I wasn't sure. My vice was cigarettes.

Two days later, the clouds lifted and I was told it was time to head up and open the lookout. I was given a Forest Service key, a radio and a pat on the back. My equipment was jimmied up from old Boy Scout artifacts and my new Pennies work boots, so I was lucky to be hiking while the weather was fair.

The lower trail was open and easy. I moved upward with innocent enthusiasm. Then I turned a corner in the trail and found myself in a daunting landscape of steep snow fields, melt ponds and islands of alpine fir and hemlock. Following someone else's boot prints, I somehow made my way through the lower snowfields. Five hours after leaving the trailhead, I finally staggered onto the lookout catwalk and buckled into a heap.

After catching my breath, I looked around. I was immediately overwhelmed by the panorama that beheld me. It was a sight that I would never grow weary of, even now as I look back.

Ultimately, it wouldn't be the environment but the abject aloneness that would define my first trip to Green Mountain. I spent that first night isolated at 6,500 feet in a glass box. As soon as the sun and temperature dropped, I was forced into my sleeping bag to wait out the night. I somehow slept but only after overreacting to every new noise that crept in from the darkness outside the door.

When the sun finally came up, I wasn't sure whether I wanted to spend the rest of the summer among the clouds and high breezes. Could I balance my need to work and the extreme isolation I would endure as a lookout?

It turned out that Howard had given me a list of things to do in order to prepare the lookout for the summer. I immediately buried myself in these tasks. I felt my confidence build as I worked my way through jobs that required me to use some ingenuity and the resources at hand.

As I lifted each of the shutters from the windows and invited light into the old building, it took on a welcoming aura. I oiled the fire finder, swept the floors, and replaced broken panes of glass. Since I was alone, I was more careful in what I did. I figured out a way to hang out over the cliffy precipice that supported the lookout and tighten down the guy wires and check the lightning rods. I eased my way up on the roof to remove the bucket over the wood stove chimney. By the end of my first full day on the lookout, my solitude began to evolve into a real feeling of independence and energy for the job.

When I left, I was not the same person who had cautiously picked his way up to the summit several days before. I was ready to stake out my own territory, no matter what bends and turns the summer would take.

A week later, a warming and drying weather trend was forecast, so the decision was made to send me back up to Green Mountain for the summer. Historically, supplies were packed in to the lookout by mule but that year the trail was impassable to livestock due to a heavy snow pack and several major blowouts on the lower trail. This meant I would get a helicopter ride up near the lookout then hand carry the whole outfit to the top. Packing consisted of stuffing personal gear, non-perishable food, and supplies for the lookout into proper sized and weighted containers that would fit into the hold of a small helicopter.

We took off early the next morning for an awe-inspiring flight to my aerie perch. Having never flown in a helicopter, I was dumbfounded by the experience. There was still a thick layer of snow on the ridge lines and summits so the vistas and contrasts were stunning. After 20 minutes of the best ride possible, the pilot glided into a dangling helipad a quarter mile below the summit. I jumped out while he feathered the whirlybird on an outcrop and off loaded my gear. The pilot gave me a wink and told me not to worry about Sasquatches as he flew away. The crushing sound of his engines quickly transitioned into complete silence. I stood there feeling both energized and abandoned as he disappeared over the ridge. I also got to watch my sleeping bag get blown over the edge and roll hundreds of feet down the east side as a result of rotor wash. My season on Green Mountain had begun.

I spent the rest of the day hauling my stuff up to the lookout and unpacking. Howard surprised me by slipping a steak and fresh fruit into my stash. Way down below, I could see my bag at the bottom of a snowfield but it was too late to chase after it. I spent a very cold night bundled up in all of my clothes and wrapped in a paper sleeping bag full of mouse droppings. That night stretched on interminably as I was dogged by the comment made by the helicopter pilot about Sasquatch.

When I'd sifted through old lookout records down at the Ranger Station a few days before, I came across this entry by Doug Newman, Green Mountain Lookout:

"Very interesting tonight. Found out reason for "copter" in the Cub Lake region. Seems it's a Sasquatch hunt. There

was a sighting in that area and some people reported being chased by them. Big Play in Seattle Papers, and radio and an expedition is being organized to look for them. The kid here is not big on meeting one—we have nothing in common, and I'd just as soon not see one in the first place…"
14 August 1965

Doug had preceded me as the lookout by a few years and had dealt with his own demons. This unsettling note followed:

"…Had 20 people up today—17 were Indians some of whom had interesting stories regarding grandparents and the Sasquatches, or 'Wild People' when they used to live along the Suiattle." 17 August 1965

These were not reassuring thoughts as I lay awake in the darkness wondering what was lurking just outside the door. Sasquatch sightings were big news in the 1960s and I wasn't immune to the rumors and creepy stories about these supposed eight-foot, hairy mountain dwellers. Slowly the morning sun emerged over Dome Peak to the east and I was able to put my night fears away.

After a slippery trip down to retrieve my sleeping bag, I returned to the lookout and began what would be a regular routine. Get up, raise the flag, make breakfast, warm up if the sun was out, make hourly sweeps with the binoculars for smokes, take the weather, relay messages on the radio, have lunch, repeat the morning routine until dinner. Evenings meant clean up and some record keeping. I could leave the lookout for a while in the late afternoon or in foul weather to fetch water or get some exercise. In between all of this, there were a myriad of jobs to do to keep the building from falling apart after its 45 years of use and exposure to extreme weather. My thoughts returned to Newman's journal entries.

"…Had eleven visitors today and no lightning. Here it is the ninth of August and no lightning! Always before on the 9th we have had a good bust. So where is it? I had some Big Billowies rolling in over White Chuck this evening but they have dissipated and only a moderately strong wind remains. It is a hopeful shade of black to the North, however so there still is hope.

Got some good pictures of grouse tonite (*sic*) down by the spring. A mama and six kids. Could have nailed them all with rocks, but I am too humane a guy. When I get down to the cans of beans, maybe things will change... hmmm..." 9 August 1965

It figures that major attractions in such a motionless environment would be anything that moved. So it was on Green Mountain. Less than two dozen visitors that summer naturally forced my attentions to the other living organisms on the mountain. My high powered binoculars allowed me into the lives of coyotes, deer, bear, goats, grouse, ptarmigan, pikas, marmots, and even a wolverine. Predatory birds, including a Golden Eagle with a nest not 100 yards away, rode the air currents nearby while keeping an eye on the ground dwellers. Other winged scavengers roved the ridgelines looking for leftovers. Ravens were the most obvious.

Near the lookout were more low profile fauna including voles, mice, pack rats, marmots, and my favorite, a chipmunk I named Juanita. Daily, Juanita would skitter up on my shoulder, snatch and stuff three raspberry jawbreakers into her cheeks and head for her winter stash. More from Newman:

"Another interesting day. Started it off by spotting two bears and a pair of coyotes this morning down the hill on the Downey Creek side...The bugs were as bad as they've been all summer. The flying ants hatched and swarmed all over everything. ..." 8 September 1965 – Newman

As it turned out, the dominant species of wildlife atop the mountain that I had the misfortune to discover were the insects. Not just an itinerant few but swarm after swarm. Squadrons of ants, no-see-ums, horse flies, deer flies, mosquitoes, and other winged pests that only came in multiples dashed visions of sunny hours on the catwalk. The biggest surprise were the thousands of lady bugs that came to the summit to make more lady bugs and coat every surface to the point where walking about was a delicate operation.

Coping with the isolation was rough, especially since I had so few visitors that summer. Several things helped keep me sane. Living at 6,500 feet meant exceptional radio reception. I had taken a decent radio with me and could pick up hundreds of stations on the AM dial. Filling the night was Wolf Man Jack coming from XERF, a 250,000-watt station 1,500 miles away out of Cuidad, Mexico. He had apparently been banned from the California airways so I got a steady stream of uncensored talk and diverse music every night. In contrast, I could pick up the Gospel Hour from Canton, Ohio and every local station available. As a child of the '60s there was always music in the background, so this helped me stay connected.

Besides for daily business and infrequent visitors, the only other conduit for human interaction for me was the lookout hour. Every night at 8:00, if there wasn't fire traffic, all of the lookouts in the region could chatter with each other on the Forest Service radio. There were faceless voices coming my way from all directions, including Desolation Peak Lookout up in the North Cascades. We'd exchange recipes, bad jokes, and stories from the day. Doug Newman, in his notes, captured the influence of these long distance relationships:

> Melissa on Dillard Point is groovy chick. A feminine voice
> has penetrated the wilderness and morale is up 200%. Now
> what does she look like? Mean question. Roger and out.
> Four visitors today. 27 July 1965 – Newman

Even though it was a very dry summer, I experienced only one or two lightning storms. On both of those nights, I spent several hours on my insulated stool as electricity danced around the metal parts of the lookout. About mid-summer, a major fire blew up at the base of Green Mountain. Started by a smoker in a very parched landscaped, the fire raced up hill through old timber and fresh clear cuts in no time. It was several hundred acres in size before I could even see it and someone else had reported it by then. The Mount Baker Forest meteorologist was flown up to the lookout and we took turns taking weather readings every half hour, for 24 hours a day for a week. At one point, we asked for some extra food. The Fire Boss had fresh chicken and several gallons of canned peas and peaches flown up, which was wasted after having been opened and unrefrigerated. On the same flight, I had asked for some cigarettes and was treated to another example of Howard's wry sense of humor. Instead of a carton of Camel filters, he made sure a rolling machine and a can of Bugler were delivered for me to struggle with. I mostly quit smoking by the end of the summer thanks to the effort it took to roll a decent smoke.

As my summer moved along and I built my own history on Green Mountain, a story about another 19-year-old lookout from another era was fun to think about. In 1948 Austin Post, who later became a renowned mountain photographer and glaciologist, was sitting atop Crater Mountain up in the North Cascades. He picked up what he described as a "youthful voice filled with terrible fear and fright" coming over the airways.

"Darrington Ranger, Darrington Ranger, there's a red headed woman up here and she says she is going to spend the night. What'll I do? What'll I do?"

Such was the plea from the Green Mountain lookout. According to Post, the District Ranger was up to the occasion.

"Son, the first prerequisite of a Forest Service Guard is self-reliance. The Service looks forward to your upholding our traditions with fortitude, perseverance, and valor."

As it turned out, the young fire watch locked the woman in the lookout and spent the night huddled in the rocks below.

Etched in my mind are my own memories of low flying jets buzzing the lookout, depressing days trapped in cloud banks, sunrises and sunsets, star shows, counting the craters on the moon with the naked eye, occasional visitors including my father and uncle, and a requirement to be conservative in what was provided in and around the lookout. The stark separation from the mainstream world was amplified by the necessity to be resourceful and less dependent on the trapping of the culture I was used to. There was no faucet to turn on water, especially hot water. The toilet was a box overhanging a rock outcrop 50 yards away. The nearest grocery or hardware store was four hours away by trail and truck. The heater in the building was an old pot-bellied stove with little wood to burn. My world was expansive and introspective, raw and rich.

I was finally released in early September as the clouds rolled in and the temperatures dropped. I put up the shutters, capped the stove flue, mouse-proofed what I could and headed down. The lookout diminished in size as I looked over my shoulder for some final glances upward. After a summer of looking below the horizon for my connection to the terrestrial world, my perspective was now upward and outward.

Sulphur Mountain Horse Tale

Predicaments and entanglements find a way to corkscrew their way into your life while working in and around the back country. If you're driving around in your U.S. Forest Service rig or walking a trail sporting the Forest Service logo then people naturally seek you out to rectify all manner of problems. This is not necessarily a bad thing. It keeps the job lively and makes for good stories back at the ranger station.

Some years ago, I was patrolling the campgrounds up the Suiattle River northeast of Darrington. It was a humdrum day until a group of unhappy campers waved me down to lodge a complaint. They had submerged their beer in the creek the night before to keep it cool when a bear happened by with a penchant for something foamy. The group stood by helplessly as the bear systematically punctured each beer can and sucked the contents dry. When the bear was done, nothing remained of the half rack of beer but crushed cans and bear slobber. I imparted as much empathy as I could but was in no position to hunt down this bear and issue a stern warning, especially if it had a big head from the night before. We discussed the pros and cons of bear proofing a camp as I edged my way out of the conversation. My flimsy excuse was there were toilets to be cleaned and my day was short. Little did I know the emergency that lay ahead.

As I was leaving the campground with an eye toward finishing my rounds and heading into town for my own beer experience, a frantic hiker flagged me down at the nearby Sulphur Mountain Way trailhead. She reported that she had been leading her horse up the trail when it failed to negotiate a tight spot and had fallen head over heels down trail about twenty five feet. The horse was okay, albeit cut and shaken. The woman tried for several hours to get her horse back on the trail but the physics of the situation were working against both her and the horse. The trail was cut into a steep bank that fell off sharply into a creek bed and the foliage was thick with large rocks blocking an easy exit. Woman and horse were in a real pickle and I was being asked to step up with some sort of resolution.

My only experience with anything similar was the memory of gruesome stories told about horses that had fallen off trails in the deep back country and were entrapped in an impossible situation or too injured to move. This usually took place during the fall High Buck Hunt when hunters took to the hills with inexperienced horses, very large weapons, and too much alcohol. The solution, unfortunately, was to release the horse from its misery by a bullet to the head. This was the merciful thing to do but it left a huge problem for the Forest Service—what to do with a dead and soon to be rotting half-ton beast deep in the wilderness. The simplest method was to move along the decomposition process by dynamiting the poor creature into many smaller more manageable parts. From there, some components could be buried with the rest left to nature. This image was swirling through my head as the owner led me a half-mile or so to the scene.

Upon arriving, I could see a very large horse below the trail looking up at us woefully. I am not a horseman but had been around horses and mules enough to know that I had no idea what to do. It was time to call Howard.

Howard Barstow was the Fire Control Officer for the ranger district I worked for and was adept at many things. For one, he had his own small farm and kept horses. He was also a horse hunter and worked with mule packers for years on various back country projects. Thankfully, he was in the office when I called and said he would be up in an hour to see what could be done. He was probably rolling his eyes as I described the situation thinking I was pulling his leg. The trail the horse tumbled over was only about a mile long and was not built for horse travel. There was no rational reason for anyone to be riding a horse up the trail, so he must have thought he was the butt end of an elaborate prank. He would know because he was often the perpetrator of inspired practical jokes and horseplay himself. He once told me what great fun it was at fire camps to initiate new firefighters by lighting up their paper sleeping bags as they dozed away in an exhaustive slumber.

It was now fairly late in the day and the weather was turning toward rain. The woman, the horse, and I spent the time staring at each other wondering who was the superior species, gender, or other hierarchical designation. Light jokes were not in order, nor were stories of failed horse rescue attempts. I kept up my end of the deal by exuding enough false male confidence to last until Howard arrived.

It was a good thing I wasn't pulling any shenanigans with Howard because he showed up in a foul mood. This, being a Friday, was his day to slip out early and dip his fishing line in the Sauk River. I had just stuffed a cork in his stress reducer.

Once he showed up, though, his compassion for horses and his patience with me prevailed and we started to work out a solution. Our first strategy was to see if we could walk the animal up the slope he had fallen. Howard's job was to lead the horse by the bridle and mine was to grab its tail and provide some kind of stability. We worked our way down beside the horse. Howard soothed him with horse talk as he adjusted the bridle.

On the count of three, Howard tightened up his grip on the harness and headed the horse uphill. I followed along like a caboose, holding the tail to help steady the horse. We made it about fifteen feet up the slope only to have the horse panic, pull away from Howard, and sidestep its way back down to our starting point. I was able to jump out of the way but only by a whisker.

We tried this approach twice more but the poor horse was not able to commit itself to the final steps up and onto the trail. Each time we neared the outside edge of the trail, the horse would panic and down we'd slide to the creek bottom. The animal at this point was near exhaustion and we weren't in much better shape. It was time to consider other options.

There were three: we could either find another way out, lure the horse up on the trail with some goodies, or the horse would have to join its ancestors on that big open range in the sky with no fences.

We decided on a new trail. I traipsed back to my rig and grabbed a variety of hand tools and we set about clearing a path upstream at an angle toward the existing trail. It was nearing dark when we were able to open a rough enough trail to allow the owner to lead her horse cautiously up the rudimentary path. Fortunately for all, this worked.

In the end, the horse and owner plodded back to the trailhead and headed home. Howard missed his date with a steelhead but could look his own horses in the eye without guilt. I found my bunk, a beer, and pondered what the next day might bring.

Mount Pilchuck

THE MOUNT PILCHUCK TRAILHEAD STARTS HIGH and continues upward without letup over the three-mile hike to the summit. The mountain itself is a lovely outcrop that occupies 5,343 vertical feet of space on the western edge of the North Central Cascades. It can be seen from almost any point along Interstate 5 driving north from Seattle and represents the closest the average commuter will ever come to the Cascades. Those interested in more than the distant view will find a mountain full of contrasts.

A trained eye will notice that the westerly and southern flanks have been heavily logged over the years and are choked with dense stands of second growth fir and hemlock. These extensive thickets represent efforts at both reforestation and nature at work repairing itself after unabated timber harvesting. To add insult to injury, a large section on the northwest corner was leveled in the 1960's to accommodate a new ski area that never actually materialized due to shaky financing and an inconsistent snow pack. What's left of this enterprise are half built concrete towers, large cables that lead off to nowhere, and a previously forested and subalpine landscape trying to heal itself.

In comparison, the northern margins of the mountain are reserved as a State of Washington Natural Study Area because of the unique plant communities that exist there. The core of the study area is riddled with steep rock slopes, pretty little lakes, and snowfields that persist until the end of July. When the grab for wood fiber came many decades ago, the trade-offs of the costs of roads and access versus board feet of salable lumber was seemingly not worth it in this lofty setting. The value added now is the availability of a pristine and protected mountain ecosystem within spitting distance of the fast food outlets down the road in Granite Falls.

Bisecting the northwestern edge is a long and windy road that leads anyone with some patience up to a king sized parking lot nestled in at 3,000 feet. The novel thing about this road is that it starts out graveled and is riddled with a washboard surface until about 2,000 feet where it then turns to asphalt. Both the sensibilities and the undercarriage of the car are assaulted for many miles only to be replaced by a smooth ride and welcome relief at the end. Why the upper half of the road was paved in lieu of the bottom is a mystery that only the Department of Natural Resources and the Forest Service can explain. Either way, the traveler arrives in a state somewhat rattled but ready to hop out and take on the mountain.

For many hikers, and there are many hikers, this is an opportunity to actually scale a real mountain, stand on top, and attain a sense of accomplishment. The hike itself is just strenuous and exposed enough in places to give the illusion of real mountaineering for the uninitiated. On a hot summer day, three hundred people with innumerable dogs will attempt to bag the peak, which makes for a congested ebb and flow. This includes every manner of hiker. Many approach the ascent with a certain amount of nonchalance. Over the years, this has led to a disproportionate number of deaths, injuries, and lost persons dressed in whatever they threw on for breakfast.

As many people begin the ascent, there is often no evidence of water, food, or anything resembling emergency gear or extra clothing, even in large groups. Everyone is equipped mainly with a leap of faith. The groups come in waves.

Early morning is given over to mostly experienced hikers that get up and back rapidly and are out to beat the rush. Up next are the folks who have had breakfast, coffee and their paper, checked to see if the sky was clear, then moseyed on up for a leisurely climb. Lastly, up comes the edgiest bunch. These are the ones who come late because of the previous night's hangovers and are often seen carrying nothing more than a six-pack, radio, and chips. This is the cut-off jeans and backwards baseball cap crowd. Many from this last queue don't actually make the summit but have a fine time settling in for a beer somewhere below with a good enough view.

Nowhere is crowding more acute than atop the summit. Some unique boulder hopping and a steep ladder climb deliver the intrepid hiker to a renovated fire lookout. Once on top, the hardy mountaineer gets to share the view and very limited space with an oversized gathering of his or her best friends. There is adventure and some risk to all of this, which has great appeal to a mostly sedentary American public.

The vertical landscape and the interlacing trail that intersects it are alluring. The upper slopes can be stunning, especially in the fall. These open reaches of jumbled granite rock fields are laced with stands of mountain hemlock, Alaska cedar, and heather bound hummocks. As the clouds lift, seemingly endless drifts of mountainous ridges and peaks head off to the north and east. The top of Mount Pilchuck provides a great look inland to a designated wilderness area and roadless back country of the Central Cascades. *Oohs* and *aahs* and photo ops abound if the clouds are cooperative. If the summit is socked in, then the only view is downward or in the imagination.

Walkers looking for an alpine escape will find it on Mount Pilchuck. Loneliness will not be part of the experience, nor will the thrill of wilderness route finding and animal encounters. If the dogs don't chase off any native fauna, then loud conversations will. The biggest challenge might just be finding a private place to get rid of the morning coffee. Ranger trips looking for garbage and toilet paper are quite rewarding.

The whole trail corridor is laced with the detritus of human throwaways and clean-me-ups. Deposits of these delights can be found with little effort behind the curtain of brush and large trees that line much of the lower trail and tree clumps up above.

If none of this bothers you, then by all means make your ascent of Mount Pilchuck. Pull off the freeway, aim for the region's highest parking lot and proceed uphill with a song in your heart and the biggest plastic bag you can find in case of the inevitable rain.

A Second Look at Heather Lake

UNIQUE EXPERIENCES IN THE MOUNTAINS are sometimes unexpected and often sublime. Heather Lake, on the lower flanks of Mount Pilchuck, is a small lake that rests on the northwest side of the mountain. It is one of many overused middle elevation lakes that pocket the western slopes of the Cascades. It lies at 2,450 feet and is surrounded by fairly dense foliage on two sides with rock fields and wetlands on the other quadrants. The hike up is short but steep enough to get the heart rate up. The access trail travels over a time-worn logging road for several miles then morphs into a beaten out pathway near the lake basin. Underfoot is a rocky tract that reflects the dominant geology of Mount Pilchuck.

For most of the way, the trail corridor snakes through old second growth forests with massive cedar stumps standing guard along the edges. The understory plants are leggy, infrequent and starved for sunlight. All things considered, there would be very little potential charm left in making this trip. Yet, a trip to clear trail and patrol the lake turned into a fine experience.

The clouds were low and obscured the bulk of Mount Pilchuck as I prepared to head out from the Verlot Ranger Station early on a quiet Monday morning in July of 2010. I was the back country ranger for the area and the upkeep of Heather Lake was my responsibility. Gazing upward toward the summit provided plenty of information on what lay ahead. A layer of marine air owned the midsection of the mountain so I reckoned this to be another typical workday with no distracting views toward the skyline.

A short drive to the trailhead led to the usual pre-hike rituals in the parking lot. Park nose out and block the tires. Pull out shovel, Pulaski, plastic garbage bags, saw, and a map of the area. Check the pack for rain gear, lunch, dark glasses, extra clothes, ditty bags full of small stuff, butt pad, first aid kit, extra food, and hat. Turn on the Forest Service radio, tuck away truck keys and wallet, double lace the boots, lock the truck, and get going. Return to the truck to get some forgotten item remembered fifty yards up the trail.

Looking skyward did nothing but confirm that this was going to be anything but a drippy, cloudy day. This is the case more often than not on Mount Pilchuck, one of the wettest spots on the western slopes of the Cascades. The trail immediately steered itself off into dense forest, the floor of which had been denied direct sunshine for ages. Did I need my headlamp? Was I foolish to carry that pair of dark glasses? My primary distraction was stumbling over loose rocks and slipping on exposed roots that had been polished by many years of booted footfalls. There were no real vistas, flitting birds or gurgling riles to provide distractions. The dominant posture was head down, feet forward.

After several miles of walking, all the while tossing branches and large rocks off the trail along the way, there was a subtle change. The pathway flattened out, the understory thickened and there were openings in the canopy. The backdrop began shifting from tired old monoliths to silver firs and smaller hemlocks. A stream could be heard off to the side and there was a sense its source wasn't far away. At one point, the trail dropped into what was—by all geological accounts—a classic glacial lake basin. Adding to this welcome shift in terrain was an openness where the clouds were now thinning and lifting and light intensity was increasing.

After another quarter mile, mounds of heather growing over exposed rock began to dominate the landscape. A quick dip in the trail opened into a V-shaped window that led to a route around the craggy reaches of the lower mountain. More walking was required to access the lake, but once there, it was like my vision had been restored. Openness soon prevailed along with grand views of the surrounding cliff systems. The foundation for all of this was the lake itself.

On this day, the lake surface was catching what sun it could and converting it into reflected images. Inverted reprints of what stood above could be seen amidst the mild ripples on the lake. Upside down snowy cliffs and elongated fingers of brushy chutes were quite distinctive in the mirrored display. Framing all this were floating mats of horsetail and reeds growing in from the edges. Adding a special garnish was a pair of Golden Eyes cruising around the lake diving for small fish and periwinkles.

After a round of cleaning campsites and fire rings near the outlet stream, I felt a strange sensation on my shoulder—sun. Yes, the clouds were dissipating and light was pouring through. In the Cascades, moisture collects in the form of drifting clouds that are often wispy and dispersed over ridgelines and spurs. Blue is revealed as the billows of white release their grip on the vertical landscape and dissolve into nothing. As you stare at this phenomenon, it always appears as if these light clouds are backing away and being absorbed into the surrounding trees and rocks. It's the ambient moisture that remains that helps nurture evergreen trees in this region, with each needle capturing millions of molecules of mist. With the direct sun, the lake basin had a different feel to it. The light brought promise and elevated my spirit. Reflection and shadow became part of the nearby fabric. It was time to circle Heather Lake.

Because of heavy usage, the Forest Service had wisely built a loop trail around the lake. Some of it is on boardwalk, some in rocky terrain, and some through stands of slide alder and willow. All of the sections provide a nice walk through mixed terrain and keep people from jamming up in the few open lakeside spots. I liked it because it provided nice flat wandering on open ground. For those who take notice, it provides different perspectives on the lake and the overhanging landscapes.

For me, what started out as an ordinary working trip into the mountains had been enriched. It's possible to get too much of a good thing and let the extraordinary become mundane. But, as John Muir said, "New beauty meets us at every step in all our wanderings." Such was the lesson of Heather Lake.

Working Fire With Punky

SATURDAY NIGHT ALONE IN A FOREST SERVICE BUNKHOUSE can be a dismal place on a fine summer night. But there I was with nothing better to do with my time then organize my stuff for my next weeks work as the Suiattle Fire Guard. I was a sitting duck. As if on cue, Howard Barstow, the fire boss, slammed through the front door and yodeled. He was trolling for firefighters. I'd lost the obsession for fire suppression some time before so I decided to lay low. Howard would likely hunt me down anyway and conscript me into duty regardless of my impending assignment and lousy attitude.

I tried to hide in the bathroom but Howard was wise to this tactic and stuck his head in the door.

"I know you're in there. I saw your light on and now I see your shoes under the stall. Get you stuff together and get on over to the fire office. We got lightning fires up near Mt. Baker and we need your kind assistance to make them go away."

I preferred chasing small smokes to major project fires, so this might not be too bad. I also had to admit that I could use the overtime. My car was falling apart from too much time spent on gravel roads and I needed a down payment for a replacement.

I grabbed my fire pack and headed over to see what the story was. Howard spoke without looking up.

"Howdy, Hanbey. I'm going to send you up north with some local color to chase down a fire on Ptarmigan Ridge. The Baker district is understaffed and they need a boost from our side."

"Thanks, Howard, but what do you mean by local color?"

"Well, your fire is burning in a tree clump somewhere just below ridge line. You'll need a couple of fallers to drop the trees and buck them up. Punky and Milton are next on the list to go out. They've been working logging shows for enough years to know which end of the chain saw to hold. Grab a rig and pick them up at the Red Top Tavern on your way out. They should be sober by the time you get up to Baker."

"Are you kidding me? You want me to pull two loggers out of a local bar on a Saturday night, drive four hours with them bobbing around in the back seat, all to drop a tree burning in a wilderness area that probably should be left alone anyway?"

"Consider this a character builder," Howard said.

"Take the crummy, a couple of extra fire packs, the usual tools, fuel, and whatever else strikes your fancy. Check in with the fire boss at Baker. Your ETA up there should be about one o'clock depending, of course, on how long it takes to get the boys away from the Red Top. By the way, I wouldn't suggest wearing your uniform when you pick them up."

I knew I had no choice but to take these guys along. Felling large timber, especially cedar, was tricky business and I would need help from people who did this for a living. I grabbed my gear and headed out.

I parked my Forest Service rig about a block from the tavern and tried to figure out a strategy to ease these boys out as I walked towards the bar. I slipped in the back door and ran into the usual wave of smoke, stale beer, drunks yelling at each other and country western music. I made my way to the semi-safety of a barstool. I figured I could sit for spell and figure out my game plan.

Soon enough, I spotted Punky over near the pool table bending someone's ear. I decided to handle things straight on.

"Hi, Punky. Howard sent me to liberate you and Milton from all this fun and take you for a ride up north. There's fire up there with your name written all over it."

Punky looked at me through half glazed eyes.

"My, my, what do we have here? The Forest Circus sent a posse to round up old Milton and me. What do you think about them apples, Milton?"

Milton was propped up against a nearby wall with his knees locked to keep him from slipping to the floor. His response was a big smile and a burp.

"I see Milton is at a loss for words, but I can tell he's pretty darn excited," Punky shouted over the noise.

"Now why should I leave this warm little nest just to go play fireman. Besides, I'm up next on the pool table."

Great, I thought to myself, another adventure in beautiful downtown Darrington.

"Don't you care if the forest burns to the ground while you're trying to sink an eight ball?"

"Are you kiddin'? It would take a nuclear device to burn this forest down. Hell, it's been raining for a month."

"Well, all I know is that you're the lucky winners on fire standby this weekend and your time has come. Now can we get out of here?"

"Let's double check with Milton. If he can give me the square root of 81 then we're on our way. If he can't, then you get to close down the tavern with us. Hey Milty, what's the square root of eighty one?"

Milton stared at us and slowly raised his hands. He opened one fist to release five fingers then opened his other hand to reveal three fingers and a stub, the victim of a logging accident the previous year.

"Nine, that's it, Milton, you're a genius," Punky said.

I trailed my two drunken companions out the door and down the street to my rig.

"You guys need to pick up anything? We'll be up in the high country," I asked.

"Yeah, drop on by my place. There's one very important commodity we never go anywhere without," Punky said.

"Okay, lead on."

As soon as we pulled out of Punky's driveway, I figured my boon companions would fall asleep before we got two miles down the road. I wasn't far from the truth. Both were out and splayed across the seats before we crossed Sauk River Bridge on the edge of town. This was fine with me; I didn't want to deal with these two characters more than I had to. Besides, I liked driving at night in the countryside listening to oddball radio stations.

I didn't really get sleepy until I pulled off the main highway and onto the gravel road that led to the guard station on the west side of Mount Baker. At night, driving on a tree-lined dirt road was like driving through a tunnel and I got into the rhythm and flow in a hypnotic way. I'd start to drift off but would revive myself by stamping my feet and singing. An object materialized in front of me—a faint form with two shining points of light. It came at me faster than I could react then jumped back at the last second.

The deer was gone by the time I realized I almost hit it. I jammed on the brakes and slid off the side of the road. Punky and Milton ended up in a tangle of arms and legs on the floor. It was to their advantage to have been drinking, as they were passed out and very flexible in this situation.

"God damn it, Hanbey, what in thunderation are you doing. Can't a fragile thing of beauty get some sleep around here?"

"Can it Punky. I almost hit a deer, a true fragile thing of beauty. We're almost there, by the way. How you guys feeling?"

"Like warmed over dog shit. I'm going back to sleep," Punky replied.

Milton never did regain consciousness until we got to the guard station.

I pulled in to find the station bustling with energy. There were fires burning and money to be made. I elbowed my way into a small room that smelled faintly like the bar I had just left—stale smoke and greasy food.

"You must be Russ Hanbey. You bring in those two fallers from Darrington?" A voice with a uniform called from behind one of the desks.

"Yeah, but they're meditating in the back of my crummy."

"Don't make any difference. We need you to head up to the backside of Ptarmigan Ridge and knock down a smoke that's been smoldering up there in a tree clump. Here are the coordinates and fire cards for the three of you. You got fire packs, saws, and a radio?"

"Yeah, we're set. The gentlemen loggers from Darrington brought their own saws. Said they'd rather use an axe than touch a Forest Service issue saw."

"Well, can't say I blame them. Go on up to the end of road 3490, catch some winks until dawn then see if you can find this smoke. We're expecting higher humidity and gusty winds tomorrow, so take care. Call me when you set out tomorrow morning."

I eased out of the room, grabbing a cup of coffee before returning to my somnolent fire crew. An hour later, we were at end of road 3490 at about 3,500 feet. I left Darrington's finest slumbering in the back seat, grabbed my bag, and found a log to cozy up to for the rest of the night. I thought I smelled a wisp of smoke before I dozed off.

"Rise and shine, the woods are burning down," Punky's grating voice cut through my sleep.

I half opened my eyes to two other sets of eyes looking down on me. The gentlemen had recovered and were ready to go. I forgot that most loggers were up before dawn no matter how bad they felt. This was going to be a frolic for them.

I was soon rattled back to life by the sputter then roar of a chainsaw. Punky and Milton were tuning up and sharpening their saws. No self-respecting logger goes into the woods with a dull blade.

"Okay, okay, I give up, let's grab some food and get out of here," I said.

I checked in with the Fire Control office, threw on my fire pack then headed out in the general direction given by the dispatcher. I wanted to make some high ground so that I could get our bearings and possibly get a visual fix on the fire. My companions tagged along, chainsaws slung over their shoulders, fuel and a bag of equipment in hand.

We bushwhacked our way up through a clear-cut to a rocky knoll for a look around. I was the only one doing all the looking. Punky and Milton knew that the longer we took to find the fire and knock it down, the more hazard pay they would make. They were in no hurry. They were treating this like some kind of holiday with pay.

I figured that I'd have to wait until a breeze came up and things dried out before we would have a clear shot at any smoke rising. No sooner had that thought crossed my mind when I noticed the obvious blue smoke of fire over a ridge half a mile away.

I took a compass reading as we began a traverse around the draw that separated us from the spur where the fire was smoldering. I didn't want to lose our bearing on the fire. The Cascade Mountains are difficult to penetrate under the best of circumstances but I had forgotten who I was with.

Loggers spend their lives in steep, thick brush in all kinds of weather. This was a cakewalk for my companions. I was impressed by their ability to slip through the densest thickets carrying their saws, barely taking a breather along the way.

Before long, we were on the crest of the ridge looking down into a smoky stand of Alaska cedars fifty yards below. As we picked our way down, I remembered to check for the nearest possible water source and for an escape route in case the fire got out of hand.

We pulled down into the draw and immediately found not one but three trees that were smoldering away, victims of the lightning strike the previous day. I called Baker and updated them on our find.

"10-4, Hanbey. How stable does it look and are you going to need any more help?"

"Negative, the weather's calm. I'll get the Darrington hot shots to drop the trees and we'll start digging."

"Okay, be careful. Watch your back."

Punky and Milton decided to drop the trees down an open and dry creek bed that paralleled the hummock where the trees were growing. There were also a few spot fires starting to flame up around the base of the trees so we decided to work on those rather then set in a fire line.

This was a judgment call on my part and a departure from standard procedures that called for a fire line first then suppression around most fires. Exceptions were mitigated by terrain, the type of fuel nearby, and weather. In this case, the understory was moist and green and the weather was cool.

I stood back while the whine of the saws came closer and closer to their final pronouncement on the mortality of the trees. All three trees were down within an hour, falling within inches of where Punky and Milt wanted them to go. Their skill was striking.

Once the trees were horizontal, we got busy bucking up the remnants in search of burning embers. Cedars can burn internally for days, even months, so we'd have to expose and extinguish every hot spot. Like dental work, each smoky crevice in the trees had to be dug out and refilled with soil to suffocate any embers. The nearest water was half a mile away and no one wanted to hump our five-gallon water bags if we didn't need to. We put our heads down and worked without comment for the rest of the day.

Around 7:00 PM, we stopped for a conversation.

"I'm wearing out. What say we take a break, setup a camp of some kind and have some food? This fire isn't going anywhere." I said.

"Sounds good to me," said Milton who hadn't spoken two sentences all day.

"So chief, how about settling in over there by those rocks? I like a Western view when I dine," Punky said.

"Okay, let's drag the gear over there and set up shop. I'll check in with Baker."

While I was updating the dispatcher at Baker on our progress, Punky and Milton made themselves comfortable near a fallen log at the base of the rock fall. They ripped open the C-ration boxes, spit some tobacco juice in a Pika hole nearby, and proceeded to root out every available can of grapefruit juice. Punky reached into his backpack and pulled out two plastic glasses and a Mason jar with some sort of clear liquid.

"So what's the deal? You guys going to set up a tarp or what? What about something for dinner?" I tried to sound official.

"Hanbey, relax. Camp ain't gonna be nothing more than any dry spot we can find to slip into with those useless paper sleeping bags

Uncle Sammy gives us. As for food, there's nothing worth touching in those boxes except the pound cake and these here cans of juice."

I could tell that Punky had something brewing and it wasn't coffee. I watched as they opened the Mason jar and carefully poured a thimbleful of the clear fluid into their glasses. Then they opened the juice and filled up their glasses. Milton shaved the bark off a twig and used it to slowly stir the contents as if he were doing a science experiment. He pulled the twig from the glass and handed it to me for a whiff.

"Nectar of the gods." Milton actually spoke again. He must have been getting excited.

I breathed some in. My eyes began to water and my nose started to run.

"My god, what is this stuff? Paint thinner?"

Milton smiled at Punky and took a sip. His reaction was different than mine. He closed his eyes, rolled the fluid around in his mouth, and swallowed hard. He put his hand to his chest and said a prayer: "Over the land and over the sea, curse of the castrated dog on thee."

Punky let out an amused snort and drank his glass in one gulp. He jumped up, bent over half way, did a small jig, and let out a series of rebel yells that made me look over my shoulder to make sure no one was watching.

"What is this poison?" I said.

"Well, can you keep this under your hat?" Punky asked with childlike innocence.

"Hey, I'm off duty. Tell me something I don't know."

"This nectar is the product of Milty's Uncle O.C. Makes it himself out there near the fair grounds in Swede Heaven. Of course, he keeps forgetting to ask permission to brew this up."

I was fascinated.

"You mean this is moonshine?"

"Well you might call it that. I think he makes it during the day, though. Want to try some?"

I thought it over. We had worked our allotted 12 hours for the day. The fire wasn't going anywhere. All we had to do was sit on it for the night. Of course, drinking was heavily discouraged at fire camps. Too late for the Darrington contingent—they were already pouring their second glass. I wanted to know how it tasted.

"Okay put a touch in my water cup here and give me a can of juice."

I mixed up my drink and took another sniff. It still smelled like turpentine but there was a faint seductiveness to it. I took my first sip. My lips began to burn then the roof of my mouth and throat as the liquor worked its way down. I put my hand to my chest and massaged my sternum as the ball of fire seemed to lodge itself somewhere between my lungs. I was speechless.

A minute later, I began to feel this warmish glow move up my spine and into a dormant cavity in the base of my brain. An hour later, I was in a semi-prone position with my face to the sky and my back in a perfect little nest of fir needles and duff. Punky was throwing out a barrage of dirty jokes and Milton was chuckling at each contribution. I hadn't felt this relaxed in ages. I also knew I was getting drunk but was past the point of caring.

After another half hour, I needed to relieve myself and so began the long journey from a sitting to standing position. I tried to jump up but was greeted with a head rush that knocked me back on my rump. My next tack was to pull myself up slowly using nearby branches. This worked to get me on my feet, but finding a clear path to the backside of a log somewhere was going be a different kind of test.

I noticed that Punky and his sidekick had moved on down by the fire and were huddled in front of some burning embers.

"What the hell you guys doing down there?" I bellowed.

It was easier to yell than talk in my normal voice. Whoa, I thought to myself, am I in trouble.

"We're having a weenie roast, you want a doggie?" Punky offered.

"Want a doggie? What are you yammering about? Is that some kind of Tar Heel instant food?"

"I ain't no Tar Heel. My grand daddy's from South Carolina not North Carolina. We're cooking round steaks, you know, hot dogs, over this pleasant little fire the good lord has provided for us. Come on down."

I tried to figure out in my haze where they had gotten hot dogs. They'd probably hauled them up with their supplies. These guys were resourceful.

"Why sure, I do believe I'll indulge myself in one of those delicacies," I said.

I stood up to head toward the fire but that was the end of my trek. I felt gravity suck me back to the ground. I passed out before I could stretch out my legs.

Sometime during the night, I felt fingers of cold air dig into parts of my body. I was half aware that it was dark and quiet and that someone had laid a sleeping bag on top of me. I didn't feel like moving anymore than it took to loosen my bootlaces and tuck the bag in around the cold spots. I buried my nose in the paper fabric and went back to sleep.

"Hanbey, this is Baker. You copy?"

I could faintly hear the crack and pop of the radio. I also smelled damp smoke. I thought it might be raining but wasn't sure. I couldn't pull my head out of my bag. I was in genuine pain.

I also knew I had to check in. I was relieved to find the radio in my pack nearby and pulled it into the bag with me. It was, indeed, raining lightly.

"10-4 Baker, this is Hanbey, go ahead."

"Just checking in on your fire and get a read on the weather. You should have called me before you started working this morning."

Both guilt and nausea swept over me. Not only had I gotten drunk on the job but I had to massage the truth a bit.

"We worked late and haven't dug in yet today because of the rain. It's cold, wet, and misty up here. This fire isn't going anywhere."

This, fortunately, was the truth.

"Okay, expose what you can to the weather and stick around for another twenty-four hours. By the way, make sure them fallers don't fall into a glass of moonshine. Check back with me at four o'clock after the afternoon weather report."

I felt that I had been blessed. I was in no condition to work for a couple more hours. The weather was doing the work for us. Punky and Milton must have sensed they'd have another full day and a half to do about three hours of work and were rolled up in their tarps under a tree. I was getting soaked but felt I deserved the discomfort. Saving these asbestos forests from the ravages of fire was someone else's passion—not mine. I rolled over just as a small flow of ice cold water dribbled down my neck.

The Outstretched Arm

I'D CRUISED BY THE CAMPSITE EARLIER en route to a trailhead down stream. As I drove by, I noticed a small white car with its passenger door open facing the road. I backed up and pulled into the mouth of the camping area and could hear music coming from the car. I figured someone was nearby, probably off in the brush taking a leak. I didn't enter the camp, not wanting to be intrusive and decided I would stop by on my way back.

After checking the Goat Lake trailhead nearby, I returned. The car was the same as before, music blaring, door open. I tentatively got out of my truck and called out to see if anyone was around. Things didn't seem right, so I decided to take a closer look.

Scattered around the car were half a dozen empty beer cans. There was some junk on the picnic table and the fire ring was cold. It was still sunny out, but it wasn't cheering things up. The whole place was eerily empty of the presence of human beings.

At the edge of the campsite was the stump of a large Douglas fir. I peeked around it and there he was. Lying on his back, slightly downhill, was a motionless man with his left arm outstretched in a supplicant position. Looking closer, I noticed a curled hand opened slightly to the over story of branches. Dappled light streamed in from above and touched the fingers.

I called out several times. No response. My heartbeat accelerated as I moved closer. I could see that the man wasn't moving, wasn't breathing. A gun lay across his chest.

I barely breathed as I stepped forward. I forced myself to look at his face. There wasn't much remaining. A bullet had found its way up through his mouth and exited with his life.

I backed off, feeling sick. The man's death filled the atmosphere with its absoluteness. It was real and unconditional.

The music continued to shriek out in the background. I thought I would know how to act in a situation like this. All I was doing now was reacting. I was sure I needed to leave things as they lay and to reach out for help. I was able to catch my breath as I slipped into the cab of the truck to call the Ranger Station.

"Verlot, this is Hanbey."

"This is Verlot. Go ahead."

I was relieved to hear Marissa on the other end. I knew her to be experienced, intellectually organized, and unflappable.

"Marissa, you'll need to call the Sheriff's Office. I'm at a possible crime scene with a fatality."

I tried to select my words carefully. I was upset and knew there were many people in the area who could pick up this broadcast on their radios. Of most concern to me was the radio at the Ranger Station next to the public information desk.

Marissa asked me several relevant questions, as I knew she would. She wanted to gently confirm if there was a death, my location, the license number on the car, and several other items. She told me she would call the Sherriff and activate a response.

After the call, I stepped outside and tried to cope with the reality that there was a deceased human being not 20 feet away. I kept checking the outstretched arm. Had it moved? Was this person going to stand up and face me? Was I in danger? Was anyone else nearby? The gun on his chest looked to have been placed there. To my untrained eye, it looked like a Luger or target-shooting model and not one of those small handguns you see on primetime television.

Then I remembered something. Just before driving by this campsite the first time, I had a close encounter with an oncoming truck. The small red truck had swerved out of its way to miss me. Inside were an older man and a passenger, both their faces obscured by baseball hats. I remembered some sort of mining insignia on the door of their old truck. I was also struck by the freshly created swerve marks on the road as I drove on. These guys seemed too old and serious to be high-tailing it up the road for the fun of it. For what it was worth, I relayed this information on to the Ranger Station to be passed on to whatever Deputy Sheriff might be driving up the same way these guys were driving out.

Marissa checked back and said that it would be awhile before the police or the local EMTs would show up. Such was life working in back country. Everything was an hour and a half away.

Now it was just the outstretched arm and me. I wasn't sure what to do with myself. Proximity to this death was unsettling.

I knew it was too early for the Deputy Sheriff to find his way up to this site but I kept a hopeful eye on the road. I checked every car as it approached. As people drove by, it seemed odd they had no clue as to the gravity of my situation. Along the freeway, we all glance over at accidents with morbid curiosity. Out here, nothing was out of balance for these folks beyond the sight of a parked Forest Service truck with an oddly distracted driver.

As time dragged on, I tried to piece together the bigger picture. Had the beer cans lying around played into the events? The car was in rough shape and loaded with garbage. Was the owner on the down and out? There was no tent, cooler, folding chairs, clothesline, or other things that typically go along with camping out. He was dressed in jeans, flannel and a light coat. My motionless companion had not occupied this site for its intended purpose. He had come here to die.

The Deputy Sheriff finally showed up and took over. After he confirmed the death and did a cursory check for the man's identification, he began the pro forma task of documenting the details of the scene. Unlike me, he seemed able to separate himself from the gruesome reality of the situation and proceed objectively.

Since he was too remote for his radio to work, he asked to use my Forest Service radio to call in his initial findings.

"Verlot, this is Deputy Johnson. Call my office and relay the following information. We have a deceased white male, name of John

Doe. Vehicle is a White Geo, license plate number XYZ123. Contact the Medical Examiner and have her arrange for a confirmation of this incident."

I was relieved others were taking over but I still needed to stay close so the Deputy Sheriff could use my truck for communication. He proceeded to analyze the scene, gather evidence, and make notes. After I filled out a detailed account of what I had seen on a form he provided, he put me to work helping him look for evidence.

He determined that our victim had most likely consumed 12 cans of beer prior to his demise. We found 11 cans in his car and a twelfth over the bank with a bullet hole in it. He also found his gun case with a stash of bullets in a plastic container. When he studied the .22 pistol, he saw that three bullets had been engaged but the last one was jammed in the barrel. This could mean that the first suicidal bullet did not kill immediately and the man was cognizant enough to fire off another round. Did he look back on his life at that moment? Did he regret his decision?

We also looked for the spent bullet casings, which were found five feet away and to the left of the corpse.

It had been three hours since I first arrived on the scene and I was ready to go. The medical examiner was due soon, so I backed out and started up the road. I wasn't a quarter mile away when she passed me. I waved her down and directed her to the obscure campsite. She was lost, this not being part of her usual rounds through the cities and suburbs of Snohomish County.

As I separated myself from the mayhem, I still felt my stomach tied in a knot and my mind wandering. The vision of the outstretched arm had lodged itself firmly in my consciousness—everything else was peripheral.

I stopped by the station on the way home and thanked Marissa for her rational calmness. I moved on down the road, but my mind stayed planted in that oppressive campsite along the unpaved road to Goat Lake.

Alone on the Edge

A GRAVEL ROAD WAS WORKING ITS MAGIC ONCE AGAIN. I was headed away from town and the sense of separation was immediate. I opened the window of the truck to let leafy, dusty wind fill the space around me. With my left arm dangling out the window, I took a deep breath of ripe air and smiled. I was headed for Green Mountain.

It was my fifth summer working with the Forest Service and I knew the area well. I was to spend my workweek tending to the lookout and patrolling several remote back country areas. It was late morning when I made the trailhead so I decided to head directly for the lookout and clean the lakeside campsites on the way out. The hike was uneventful with the weather remaining fair until I reached the summit. Once there, the usual afternoon updrafts were buffeting two sides of the lookout with a vengeance. Horsetail clouds were forming on the horizon. This was not a harbinger of good weather.

Stepping into the lookout provided a marked contrast to the heavy winds outside. On clear days, the inside of the lookout was not only calmer but twenty degrees warmer. After a long haul, it was pure pleasure to drop my load, sit on the cot, and stare for awhile.

I fiddled around doing odd jobs, ate dinner, and watched the sun drop. As I settled in, I briefly thought about what Hank, my boss, said about working alone in the back country: you're not always in control but you can depend on your abilities and trust that your instincts will carry your through.

At dawn, I lay back in my sleeping bag and listened to the air currents sweep over and under the lookout. The sound was melancholy and reminded me of other times and places. Outside, the world had become grey and indistinct.

Standing on the catwalk drinking my morning coffee was not unlike standing on the prow of a ship at sea. It was dramatic and bracing but it also signaled the start of several days of dreary weather in the middle of summer. The barometer had dropped, the temperature had dropped, the clouds had dropped and the lookout was soon enveloped in a blanket of white. I decided I'd gear up and follow a way trail down from the lookout and patrol northward into the Glacier Peak Wilderness.

The trail along the ridge was really only a glorified game trail and seldom used. Hunters used the steep and remote path in the fall and back country types used it to start in on a popular alpine traverse to Snowking Mountain.

With this in mind, I picked my way several hundred feet down through a sea of false hellebore, a leafy plant capable of collecting and diverting large amounts of water to its root wad. It also soaked anyone who pushed his way through, especially in misty weather. After ten minutes, I was wet from my waist down but paid no attention. The combination of wool and raingear would begin drying as soon as I stepped away from this sodden garden. I pressed on then started climbing a knob running laterally to the main ridge of Green Mountain.

I relished coming up over these ridges and examining what lay in front of me. The landscape changed every fifty feet in this country and there were always surprises and something unique to study. Remembering that I was on the job, I decided to check the basin below for fire rings and garbage. If there was nothing obvious, I could stay high and cross over the upper end of the basin to the next spur. Then, I'd climb up to the ridgeline and drop down to a hidden lake on the other side of the mountain. Once there, I'd clean fire rings and gather up garbage, if need be.

I pulled out my binoculars and made a visual sweep of the basin below. I hadn't heard of any hunters coming into the area last fall so I didn't expect to see any clutter. As I studied the fragile turf below, I was relieved to find it unused and rested.

My route continued up through a narrow gap with narrow shoulders and loose rock to a low pass above. I wasn't concerned about the hazards—they always looked worse then they were. Slowing down and making sure that each foot and handhold was secure minimized the risk. An intuitive feel of how to glide through touchy terrain was my best tool.

Though I had seen a few signs along the way, I was not prepared for the male goat perched above me. Before I knew it, he took a startled leap away and kicked off a bucketful of rocks. Each sequence of falling rocks unloosened even larger rocks. When they reached me seconds later, I only had enough time to turn to one side and dive headfirst down into the gulley as one of the bigger stones just missed me.

I thrust my arms out as I landed then rolled onto my right shoulder into a rock. The pain was immediate. I was relieved that I hadn't hit my head but I couldn't breathe very well and was face down with my feet uphill. This was one serving of good news and two helpings of bad.

Once I gathered my thoughts, it was obvious I'd have to right myself. I couldn't push myself up so I started moving my hips and knees to see if I could saddle left or right into a more secure position. I needed to get my head up and catch my breath.

Eventually I was able to give a hefty push and get into a kneeling position. The next effort required me to spin around into a sitting position. I was getting dizzy, but my last exertion allowed me to drop my legs below my waist and find a small lip on a rock to sit on. I made myself take deep, relaxing breaths. As I closed my eyes to allow my heart to stop racing, I heard the whoosh and caw of a raven sweeping over the gully. This calmed me and helped me feel grounded.

I slowly opened my eyes and began to examine my predicament. I was alone, two miles from the fire lookout, five miles from the trailhead, and forty miles from the nearest town, which was thirty miles from the nearest hospital. It was early in the day and the light rain looked likely to continue.

I carried enough gear in my daypack to camp out for several days but I was several hundred feet up a steep, loose rock gully with only one water bottle. My radio wasn't likely to reach the Ranger Station from where I sat.

My left arm and both legs were okay but my right arm felt numb and painful. I had really whacked my shoulder on my way down. A quick check revealed some cuts and scratches but nothing serious.

I surmised that I was far enough away from help that I would have to work my way out of this alone. The fallback when working alone in the back country is always self-reliance and confidence that things will work out. My first job was to get out of this gully, out of the rain, and into a sheltered spot.

I started to ease my way down the draw using my left arm and legs. The chute provided enough stable footholds that I was able to lower myself without too many anxious moments. Twenty minutes later, the gully widened and became less vertical. I started looking around for a dry spot on the wooded edge of the draw.

I spotted a down-sloping snag with a hollow underneath, crawled in, and made myself comfortable. I dug out my water bottle, some candy, and my first aid kit. I knew how hard it was to self-administer first aid and didn't have much hope on that account. I figured nothing was broken but my shoulder was probably dislocated or seriously bruised. Either way, I had to immobilize my arm. I jerry-rigged a sling and attached it to my body with several larger handkerchiefs and my belt.

Wondering if my pants would fall down, I started out again. I was sweating from all the effort and almost emptied my water bottle on my next drink. I sat back down again, closed my eyes and began to drift. I was startled awake by the isolation, pain, and cold. My watch said two o'clock, which was enough time to get back to the lookout in the light if I was able. It was raining harder and the temperature was creeping downward. I decided to bundle up and press on cautiously.

I pulled my radio out and made an attempt to establish contact with someone. There was no response.

I struggled to get the rain pants on that I'd regrettably taken off earlier. This required me to untie then retie my boots with one hand. I had to tighten the knots on my boots with my teeth and left hand. My boots were way too loose but would have to do. I put on my wool hat, raincoat, and a glove. The daypack went over my one good shoulder.

After a few minutes of wandering, I found a small stream flowing down from the direction I wanted to go. I knew there would be stable footing in the streambed and stepped in. Walking in the shallow water combined with the rain soon forced water into places I was not happy about. My physical effort was keeping me warm, but if I had to bivouac for the night, the pain and cold would be an issue.

At the top of the rivulet was a small snowfield which gave me access to easier terrain. I ducked in under a skirt of overhanging cedar branches and found a comfortable log to lean against. I dropped my pack, the weight of which had begun to cut into my left shoulder. I was light-headed.

I pulled my coat over my injured shoulder, tucked my pack under my legs, and readjusted my stocking hat. I loosened the sling on my arm and laid back as well as I could. Relief came quickly as my breathing and circulation got back into sync. I looked out under the canopy of branches and began to feel sleepy.

I nodded off, but was prodded awake by a stob sticking in my back. I reached behind and bent the branch in another direction and tried to relax again. I felt nauseous from the effort. My energy was ebbing.

It helped that I wasn't afraid of the mountains. I didn't see hidden dangers over every ridge and behind every tree. My relationship with these remote landscapes had evolved over the years to one of cautious comfort. I wasn't surprised that I'd startled the goat and it had returned the favor by kicking some rocks in my direction. I nibbled on some chocolate, catching a view through the mist of the outline of the lookout off in the distance.

The ridge that led to the summit of Green Mountain was the line of travel I needed to take. I looked in vain for the game trail I had come out on. I knew there were marmot runs and goat trails all over these slopes, but the dense meadow plants covered anything obvious. I would have to find a different gully and pick my way to the summit ridge. I was woozy again.

After gathering my strength for a few minutes, I grabbed a handful of blueberry bushes and pulled myself another step laterally through the brush. An upward sloping rock bed caught my eye. It was steep but looked accessible and could be my escape route. I started up with renewed confidence. Each step seemed secure. Every rock gave way to a foothold. This was working.

A half hour later, I was still climbing and angling toward the lookout that I could see off towards my left. The sun seemed to be setting over the western ridges and it was getting colder. I knew I had to get to the lookout as fast as possible.

I was finally able to tap into one of the old trails that encircled the lookout and gave me predictable footing on familiar terrain. After another ten minutes of effort, I was at the base of the building. From here, I knew exactly what to do. I'd need to grab the guy wires and swing around to some footholds that passed under the east side of the building, and pull up on the next set of wires. Up a few stairs and this would put me at the front door of the sanctuary. I did this more from habit than inspired effort and was on the catwalk in no time.

Relief swept over me. I was safe. For others, being this far from help might have been intimidating. For me, this was my home away from home having lived here as fire lookout many years before.

I dropped my pack and raingear and sat on the old bed that owned the southwest corner of the building. I forced down some water then eased down into a resting position that minimized the pain in my shoulder. I knew I needed to call in but I was too tired to make the effort. I pulled part of the sleeping bag over my shoulder, took a deep breath, and began to doze.

Sometime later, the shutters in the old building began to rattle with their wind driven hum. A gust of wind slapped the side of the lookout. I felt myself pushing back my stupor as I gained an awareness of the lookout. The first thing I noticed was the pain in my feet. I'd forgotten to take off my boots and my feet were swollen and numb. I leaned forward to loosen my laces but was pulled back by the throbbing in my arm and shoulder. I was startled by it and my lack of mobility. My condition had worsened. My body had stiffened up.

I laid back and waited for the pain to subside. I knew it was time for me to figure out what to do. I felt a twinge of despair as I considered my situation. It was time to call Hank. The lookout had a powerful radio that was set up by the bed. I reached over, turned up the sound, and adjusted the squelch.

"Whitehorse, this is Hanbey. Hank please."

I tried to make my voice as balanced as possible and not broadcast any undue urgency.

Hank kept a receiver at his home and I knew he would come on line if he heard me.

"Whitehorse, this is Hanbey, Hank please."

I hoped he would pick up instead of someone else hanging around the station.

"Hanbey, this is Janet. Hank's out bailing hay. Can this wait or do you want me to get him?"

Hank's wife was never impatient with the people working for Hank. She accepted his life with the Forest Service and tolerated random interferences such as this.

"Hi Janet, this is Russ. I'm in kind of a jam up here on Green Mountain and need to talk to Hank."

Janet didn't hesitate. She could read between the lines. Something out of the ordinary was up. Several minutes later, Hank picked up.

"Hey Russ, don't tell me you finally spotted a fire up there after all these years?"

I could tell that Hank had sensed Janet's urgency.

"Not quite Hank, I had a little run in with a goat and he won. I was near the pass to Horse Camp when a rock came down that gulley on the east side and almost hit my shoulder. I nosedived into the gulley but injured my shoulder along the way. I've also got some cuts and bruises, but nothing big. It took me most of the afternoon to work my way back to the lookout."

"Good Lord, Russ. What's going on up there? Are you really okay? Tell me the truth."

"I don't think I can move much further without some help, Hank. My shoulder really hurts."

I didn't want to sound as if I were desperate but I was beginning to feel my endurance waning.

"Okay, Russ. Do you feel like you're pretty stable in the lookout? Should I order up a helicopter?"

Hank was trying to figure things out as he went along.

I looked outside at the fog soup, high winds, and encroaching darkness surrounding the lookout.

"Well, the lookout is as desolate as it always is in foul weather. Forget the helicopter. It's too dense out there," I said.

"Russ, this is what I want you to do. Keep yourself warm, immobilize your shoulder and arm as much as possible, take some aspirin if you can hold it down and climb into your bag. Lay back and we'll be up there before you know it."

We both knew that would be four to five hours at a minimum.

"Okay Hank, I guess I don't have much choice," I said.

"Damned right you don't. You hold on and we'll be there before you can remember my middle name. Stay by your radio."

I tried to remember Hank's middle name as I fell back into a restless sleep. The light and wind were playing tricks on me again. The moaning of the shutters gave way to the swirl of darkened clouds just outside the window at my elbow. I felt a chill in the dank lookout and knew it must be later in the evening. I pulled the edge of my bag up around my nose and tugged my stocking hat down over my eyes.

"So Russ, don't you ever clean up around here? There's a mouse dropping in this here water glass."

I looked over at Hank standing near the end of the bed.

"Hank, nice you could make it. Did they have to airlift you up here?"

Hank had spread out in the middle over the years and had spent too many hours riding his desk but he could still out-hike and out-pack anyone in the territory when he had to.

The glass on the inside of the lookout fogged up immediately from the crew's accelerated effort to get up the mountain in a hurry. It was barely seven in the morning. Hank must have scoured the bunkhouse for help and had everyone on the road by four. It felt good to be surrounded by familiar faces.

Hank treated the cuts on my forehead and probed a bit around my shoulder. He confirmed my belief that it was probably dislocated and not broken. The pain was the same either way. He pulled out a large bandage and carefully immobilized my arm and upper shoulder. Everything was swollen and tender.

"So Russ, think you can wander off this Godforsaken peak or shall we fix up a stretcher?" asked Hank.

"Listen, I climbed up here with a useless arm, and I can damn well climb down. My legs are fine."

I knew I was not very convincing, but I was in no mood to be hand carried down the trail like a sack of flour.

As we started out, Hank quietly handed me his old ice axe, the one with the long wooden handle.

"I thought you might balk at being carried out of here, so I brought this for you to lean on."

"Sure, I'll give this antique a try."

I began the steep descent thinking it would be a manageable struggle. After ten steps, I discovered that each step over the next four miles would jostle and jolt my shoulder. I was glad to not be alone on this trip. The presence of my friends and the give-and-take conversation that accompanies long walks on trails would ease me through this. And it did.

Coming down three thousand feet, one excruciating step at a time almost knocked me out. I had to sit down often to regain my strength and catch my breath. It also brought me down to a different elevation where the sun was peeking through the clouds and it was summertime again.

Two hours later, I was at the trailhead and ready to go home. I gave Hank back his old ice axe, and mumbled sincere thanks.

I was shaking and sick from the ordeal of my trip down Green Mountain but I had made it and was ready to give myself over to others. I was in a haze during the trip back to the station then on to the clinic.

I remembered little about the next several hours, something about x-rays, a few stitches and then being delivered to the bunkhouse. I would be out of the mountains for awhile. I'd heal up, probably get restless then get back at it as soon as I could. The landscape I loved would remain unchanged but never static. There was always something going on up there and I was part of it. I'd be back on the edge soon enough.

Crisis at Kennedy

IN JULY OF 1976, I WAS HEADED OUT TO WORK a ten day tour as a back country ranger in the Kennedy Hot Springs area of the Glacier Peak Wilderness. I would be spending part of my time on the way up working with two trail crew guys, Mack and Whistle Pig. They usually worked alone but this time out some heavy trail work would need extra hands. Little did we know that we would walk headfirst into an unprecedented environmental event that would change life forever in the Whitechuck River Valley.

I squeezed myself into the cab of the Forest Service rig as we pulled out of the ranger station. I waited for Whistle Pig's latest litany of complaints even before we hit the road for the Whitechuck River trailhead.

"Gall darned Forest Circus. Every time I turn right, they say go left. Every time I stand up, they say sit down."

"What's your problem now, Whistle Pig?" I asked.

"I got no problem. Gall darned Uncle Sammy has the problem. I put in my request to continue working as a faller on project fires and now they say that I got to get myself re-qualified. I kindly pointed out that I been working these woods since I was a kid and I don't need a certificate to drop a tree. Screw it. I don't need the fire pay anyway. I can work weekends at the shake mill."

"So Mack, now that Whistle Pig has himself in a lather, what kind of work do we have lined up so he can find his mission in life again?" I said.

"Well, we're supposed to be bucking out some windfall and clearing tread on the first five miles of the White Chuck. We'll camp at Pumice Creek and work in both directions."

Mack wasn't dull, but he wasn't very complicated either. He knew what he knew and quietly went about his business. Whistle Pig, on the other hand, was a local with an attitude. He had learned to make up for short stature with constant talk, mostly producing hot air. Pound for pound, there was no one stronger than him in the valley, but he was a short man with a big chip on his shoulder.

Whistle Pig had grown up in Darrington. His dad was a gyppo logger and his mom a local girl. They'd married when his dad was 21 and his mom was 16, which was common practice. There were few single women at that time in Darrington, unless they were widows.

Whistle Pig's dad worked 10-12 hours a day, six days a week felling and bucking trees for local logging outfits. He went where the work was no matter the weather. His only vices were chewing tobacco and Monday night football. All of his checks went to Whistle Pig's mom, which were meager at best. After the first year, she learned to hold back money for the inevitable layoffs. Whistle Pig grew up in a world of God fearing, hard drinking, and inherently decent people.

Loggers are intimidated by little in the woods, short of wasps' nests and runaway equipment. Whistle Pig was no exception. The kind of work they do is continually hazardous, strenuous, and just plain hard. Six days a week of long hours on steep hills in lousy weather toughens the hide and the spirit. Time spent cutting trees, dragging rigging, and other heavy handed aspects of logging builds stamina and muscles that can't be produced in a gym. Whistle Pig had worked early on as a choker setter for his dad's logging operations. This job required him to run full bore all day over a logging unit wrapping heavy cables around newly cut trees to be hauled up to a landing. It was exhausting work that separated those who could log from those who couldn't measure up.

Unfortunately, with most of the big timber gone, few jobs remained. Logging was a way of life that was built on a house of cards. America's demand for cheap timber and wood fiber was rapidly depleting the supply.

The worst thing for many people in Darrington was to become dependent on the outside world. Whistle Pig was from the first generation of upper valley families that wasn't going to be able to center his life around logging. He swallowed his pride and went to work for the Forest Service working on trails and occasionally fighting fires.

I glanced down at the White Chuck River as we turned off the main road onto the spur that led 11 miles up to the trailhead. What I saw was unbelievable. The river was rolling and boiling and had turned almost black. This wasn't right, especially for this time of year. The river was fed primarily by glacier melt at its source, so it was almost always chalky white.

"Look at that, the river's changed colors, It's dirty brown. I wonder what's going on?" I said.

"No kidding," Whistle Pig said.

"Never seen anything like that," Mack said.

When we got to the trailhead, we jumped out with more eagerness than usual. Normally, we would dally at the trailhead, adjusting gear, going to the privy, putting some last minute grease on our boots. Today, we slapped on our packs, grabbed our tools, and headed out in a hurry. Even Whistle Pig wasn't complaining.

At the first bend in the trail, we stopped at an overlook to stare at the river below. Not only was the river dark and roiling but we also could see large boulders and trees being carried rapidly downstream. It sounded like distant thunder or waves rolling over on a beach.

We moved not really knowing what to expect. The trail to Kennedy Hot Springs is a typical primary access trail. It starts high above the river on a bench and heads straight up valley. After two miles, we dropped down onto a bench where the trail is constructed on a bench just below the high water mark.

"Holy Toledo, what happened here?" Mack blurted out.

Where there had been a thicket of trees and well-defined trail stood instead freshly deposited rock rubble and mangled trees. Huge, fifteen-foot wide trees were stacked in helter-skelter piles in front of us.

"Can you believe this mess? Something big time is happening upstream. What do you think we ought to do?" Mack said.

"Well Mack, I think we get to make an administrative decision. I say you guys start rerouting a temporary trail around this jam," I said.

"Not a bad idea, but what about you?"

"I think I should head on up trail to where I'll try to check in with Darrington on the radio. Then I'll keep going to see if there is any other damage and find out if any people are in trouble. Did you notice the 10 to 15 cars at the trailhead, but we haven't run into any hikers all morning?"

The Whitechuck trail was very popular. No one ever walked it either way without running into several dozen hikers or climbers.

"I'll call you in half an hour, then check in with Bernie or Howard when I get high enough on the trail to reach one of them," I called over my shoulder as I walked away.

I picked my way across the flat, sliding over boulders and trees still wet from their trip downstream. My adrenaline level was soaring.

I picked up the existing trail where it had broken away and headed up at a rapid pace. I told myself to turn it down a notch. I had a long way to go and had no idea what lay ahead. After 15 more minutes of walking, I had regained some elevation above the river. Looking for a place to call in, I nearly stepped off a 50-foot drop-off into the river. The river had caused an entire slope to collapse and, with it, another several hundred feet of trail. I found myself on an overhanging section of trail that had been undercut by a slide.

I had to scramble up and over the next 300 feet pushing my way through dense brush to bypass the slide. I was used to bushwhacking but the instability of the slope made me pause and reflect on the downside of traveling off trail alone on unstable ground. When I got to the other side I sat down, gobbled some nuts, and took a hit of water. I needed to think.

I was witnessing a major midsummer flood event in a relatively stable river valley and in fair weather. I still hadn't encountered any people. Before I left, there had been no reports of any unusual activity on or around Glacier Peak by the seismologists, the public, or rangers in the area.

It had been raining hard at higher elevations for the last three days, but this was common in early July in the Cascades. All of this would make sense later when we found out that a natural dam had built up at the base of the Scimitar Glacier three miles above Kennedy Hot Springs and burst out under its own pressure. Millions of cubic feet of water and ice flushed out and produced the pandemonium I was watching.

I did remember to radio out to Mack and Whistle Pig. I tried to tell them what I had seen. I recommended they finish clearing a simple path through the first blowout but there was no need to try and bypass the second slide. It was too precarious. The whole trail would probably need to be closed. Unfortunately, I couldn't get through to Darrington to get some guidance.

It was good talking to Mack and Whistle Pig—they were still pretty wound up. My initial energy was turning to anticipatory dread as I neared within a mile of Kennedy. On any given night this time of year, scores of people might be camped in the area. Ultimately, I knew that the forces that had created the chaos in front of me had to have come straight through Kennedy with its usual contingent of transient hikers and climbers. I did not want to be witness to a tragedy.

The trail had always followed the river on high ground at this point and crossed several small feeder stream bridges as it worked its way into the Kennedy area. For the first time in all my trips into the area, I was forced to find my way and not follow a friendly trail into camp. I went up on the hillside and bushwhacked the whole way through a thicket of silver firs, huckleberries, and other obstacles. I couldn't walk the plateau where the trail had been because of the piles of debris and multiple streams running through it.

I forced my way through one last tangle of brush and stepped out onto a small bluff. There, before me, was a gash in the landscape that used to be Kennedy Creek. Water was still flowing but now it was black and swollen. It flowed through a chasm that was easily 75 yards across and was full of twisted, massive trees and freshly deposited boulders. The devastation continued on down into what used to be the campground area. The Whitechuck River itself had been pushed 50 feet outside of its channel by the force of the deluge.

I looked to my left toward the direction of the onslaught. There could be only one source for this mayhem: Glacier Peak. Unseen and three miles upstream, this dozing volcano was the centerpiece for the wilderness tract that surrounded me. Visible or not, it was always there defining and directing life within its shadow. It created local weather, predetermined soil types, controlled water flow and was often the source of major events such as the current one.

I decided to work my way across the chasm and around to the Kennedy cabin. I tried not to think about what lay buried under the 15 to 20 new feet of new rock and mud that had arrived in the middle of the campground to my right.

I eased my way down the bluff over loose, steep soil onto the first log I came to. It was slimy, having been recently stripped of its bark. It stretched most of the way across. I worked my way over then jumped to another tortured log. From there, I was able to step onto a gravel bar and appraise my next move. I thought I heard voices, but I knew full well that streams could sound human at times. I began to push my way through some branches to another log when I saw a man.

He was on the opposite bank waving his arms wildly. He seemed to be telling me to go back but we couldn't communicate over the roar of the stream. I choose to keep going and crossed the main channel on the last available log that touched the opposite bank.

"Hello, what's going on here?" I shouted above the roar.

The man was dressed in back country clothes and looked haggard.

"Why didn't you go back when I told you!"

"I was halfway over. Why should I turn back?"

"You could have been killed. Every twenty minutes or so a tidal wave of huge rocks and trees comes down that valley. You made it through between waves," the man yelled.

"Wow, I guess I got lucky. Are you alone?"

"No, there are 14 of us trapped over here. Nobody wants to cross this mess. I think some people may have been buried by the slide."

He seemed composed enough considering what he had been through. I suggested moving up the hillside. I needed to check in with the rest of the group.

Together, we headed up through some exposed roots and heavy brush onto a rough path that led off toward the Kennedy ranger's cabin. It was unharmed but was now at the edge of the new flood plain. A larger group of people huddled under tarps. The man and I approached the group who immediately gathered around.

"Hi, my name is Russ Hanbey. I'm one of the Wilderness Rangers for this area. I stay in the Kennedy cabin. Looks like you guys have been through a tough experience. Is anyone hurt?"

A tall, lanky woman in a wool cap spoke up first.

"Wait a minute. Where's the rest of your group?"

"What group, I'm all alone," I said.

"You mean you're not the rescue party?"

I could tell these people were jumpy, so I proceeded slowly.

"I'm not a rescue party," I told them. "But I'm here to help. How long have you been stranded?"

"Last night and today. None of us have much more than our clothes, some tarps, and a little bit of food," a man in his forties said.

"We tried to get into the cabin to look for a radio, some food, and to get out of the weather, but it was locked up tight," another man from the group pitched in.

"Does anyone know about any missing persons?"

Before anyone could answer, a huge grinding noise churned its way down Kennedy Creek as the mountain released another torrent of debris. I was startled by the immensity of it all. The twenty-foot high wall of rock and mangled wood pushing its way down the stream channel was totally out of proportion with its surroundings. It looked like the stream corridor was purging itself. One mass of landscape stood still in the foreground as an equally large section moved behind it. I understood now why the group didn't want to cross the gorge and how fortunate I'd been to not get caught in one of the surges.

"That was incredible," I said to no one in particular.

"Yeah, that's been happening continuously. It's really a sight to behold," the man who'd first seen me said.

"How are we going to get out of here?" Someone else piped in.

"First, I need someone to give me a quick rundown on what has happened so far, and what you know about possible missing people."

The woman in the wool hat spoke up.

"Well, we were all standing around the main camp last night getting ready for dinner. About eight, Jacob, who was camped near the edge by Kennedy Creek, noticed that the water was rising in the creek and beginning to dribble through the campground. We all just stood there watching as more and more water began flowing over the banks into our campsites. Some of us started to throw our stuff together so it wouldn't get wet but the flow increased. Most of us were able to get some equipment packed before the campground was really flooded. As we were grabbing our stuff, we heard this incredible thunderous noise coming our way from over the brush along the creek. Then the first wave blew out the bottom of the camp area, near the outhouse. We all panicked and headed for that slope over there to see what was going to happen next. After twenty minutes, nothing big happened and we started down to get the rest of our stuff. We didn't get far. All of a sudden a massive slide came down that ripped apart the whole camp area. We couldn't believe it. For about an hour we just watched. Since the area around the cabin seemed to be out of the way, we all spent the night here. We built that fire over there, I hope that's okay.

"Don't worry about the fire. You did what you needed to do to keep warm. Did it rain last night?" I said.

"No, thank goodness. We all have plenty of clothes but only a few tents and tarps. It was a long night. We could hear the slides coming down all night. It was pretty frightening. Today, we just hung out trying to figure out if we should go across and get out. We were sure someone downstream knew what was going on and that we would be getting some help," the same woman continued "But no one came and the slides continued so we just stayed put. We feel like we're trapped. Are we?"

"Well yes and no. You can't go out the main trail without help, I can tell you that. The other trails out of here just go further into the back country, so that's a problem. How are you guys holding up?" I said.

"I'm worried that my wife and kids will think I'm hurt or lost. I was due out this morning. Can you let them know what's going on?" one man who was visibly upset asked.

"You bet. I need all your names and a contact person and number. I'm going to go up on the ridge and radio for help and ask our dispatcher to get in touch with your families."

I unlocked the cabin, got a tablet and began circulating it around. I had to get back to the issue of missing persons.

"Can anyone help me get a line on missing persons?"

"I can help you with that," said the first man I had met.

"We talked about it last night. All we know is that when everything started last night, a group of five climbers showed up. They had just come off the mountain and had all of their gear. They were on their way out but when it became obvious that they couldn't get across Kennedy Creek, they decided to head back up to try the upper crossing and left. We haven't seen them since."

And I didn't pass them on the way out, I thought to myself.

"The other problem," he continued, "is that half buried tent down there. It doesn't belong to any of us. We're not sure if there are people in it or not. We haven't been able to confirm anything because of the slides."

I knew I should check the area but it would have to wait.

"Listen, I'm going to take your list of names and go on up the hillside and call in. I'll start the ball rolling to get you out of here, even though I'm not sure it will be today. In the meantime, you can make use of the cabin and make yourselves more comfortable."

Radio reception at Kennedy was either unreliable or non-existent. I had no choice but to climb a half mile and 500 feet up a side trail to a point where communication with Darrington was more predictable. On my way up, I tried to weigh and measure what was going on. I wanted to be composed when I called in. They needed to know that this was a serious situation requiring large-scale intervention.

"Darrington, this is Hanbey. Bernie, please."

No response. I changed positions.

"Darrington, this is Hanbey, I need to speak with someone. This is an emergency."

I continued to wait, but I felt strangely elevated. Everything around me crackled with life. It was cold and breezy but I was warm from the rush. This was to be a defining moment for me, one so rich with the electricity of living that it would be seared into my memory forever. This was not my perspective at the time. I was immersed in the here and now. The radio pulled me from my reverie.

"Hanbey, this is Bernie, what's going on?"

"Bernie, I'm involved in a pretty serious situation here. I need to know if you can read me clearly."

I knew this would draw the attention of every employee in the region that was near a radio. We all half listen to our radios until we're called or something interesting happens. I was about to make their day.

"Yeah, I can hear you pretty well. What's your 10-20?"

"I'm at the call in point above Kennedy. We've got fourteen people trapped down below at the hot springs with the possibility of several others unaccounted for."

As I was saying this, it dawned on me how ridiculous this was going to seem down below at the station. Though Kennedy Hot Springs was located at 3,500 feet in a designated Wilderness area below a major glaciated volcano, it was known as an easy place to get to and safe place to be. It lay on a major access route to the Pacific Crest Trail, and was one of the main portals for climbers heading in to ascend Glacier Peak. It was also the first overnight spot for many new backpackers and the destination of hundreds of day hikers. The main attraction, of course, was the hot springs. They weren't medicinal but the temperature, location and geothermic bubbles drew the crowds.

My problem was to try and describe the gravity of the problem at Kennedy and along the trail to Bernie without being an alarmist.

"What do you mean trapped?" asked Bernie.

"An ongoing series of floods have blown out much of the Kennedy backpacker's camp and large sections of the lower trail along the river. There are stretches that are basically impassable. The trail needs to be closed immediately. Up here, these people are in their second day of being cut off and are unable to cross the flooded areas and get out. No one is hurt, but most of them have lost equipment. I also have five climbers who left the group to try the upper crossing but haven't been seen. You can check in with Mack to get more information on the lower trail, but up here everything is gone, I mean changed. It's just hard to explain without seeing it."

"10-6. Hold on."

Bernie must have been mulling over this situation, trying to shift his thinking away from the papers on his desk to this newest revelation. After a few minutes, he came on.

"Hanbey, this is Smith. Looks like a difficult situation. What are our options?"

I had already been considering the alternatives, which were few. One possibility was a helicopter evacuation. This was problematic because of the narrowness of the valley and the weather. Another choice was to hike the group out over the upper Kennedy Creek crossing then out the Whitechuck trail. This wasn't workable because it could be just as bad above and dangerous below on the main trail. Another approach would be to climb 3,000 feet up another trail to Lost Creek Ridge and travel several days out to the next drainage over. This wasn't going to work because the people were under equipped, underfed, and many were not in shape for that kind of trip. The most likely plan would be to somehow cross the river and take everyone back down the Whitechuck to the trailhead. I passed these ideas on to Bernie but I knew the final decision on our course of action would be his.

"Bernie, at this point our choices are limited. That's why I need some help up here. No one is in immediate danger, but things could unravel, especially if the weather turns back to rain.

"Okay, I'm going to grab Jim Weiman and head on up."

"Sounds good. Pass me on to Hazel so I can give her the names and phone numbers of the people stuck up here. Their families need to know they're okay."

"10-4, we'll head out of here within the hour. I'll try to get through to you from the trailhead."

"10-4. Watch for Mack and Whistle Pig along the trail. I'm going to head on up to check out the upper crossing and see if I can account for the climbers then drop back down into Kennedy."

I grabbed my stuff and headed toward the upper Whitechuck River crossing. I was concerned about leaving the group alone down below for much longer but I also needed to see if the upper crossing was passable.

The trail switch backed up very steeply, and then suddenly leveled out. It was a curiosity of nature that there would be a flat expanse halfway up a major volcanic peak. This level anomaly of geology made for rapid, albeit muddy travel. No matter, I used the gentle gradient to my advantage and moved along rapidly. Just as I was pulling into the camp area near the crossing, I ran into five well-equipped climbers heading down.

"How you doing. My name is Russ Hanbey. I'm the Kennedy ranger and I'm looking for some people who were at the hot springs last night but left for the high country."

"Well, that's us. We couldn't get across up above so we were heading down below to try there again," one man spoke up immediately.

"Things are pretty tough down there. No one has gotten out yet. I came up the main trail this morning and it's basically impassable down below."

I could see the guy who spoke was chewing on this and he wasn't smiling.

"We really have no choice but to get out. We're on a schedule and are running a day late already," the leader chimed in impatiently.

"Well, I'm sorry, but it's probably best that you join the group down below and wait for a safe escort out."

"Well, I'm sorry too, but we can get out on our own."

My line on this joyful person was that he was probably guiding a private climb of Glacier Peak and that hadn't counted on nature setting up roadblocks. This guy was losing money by being here too long.

"That's your prerogative. I want you to sign a note that states that you are leaving of your own free will against my advice. You willing to do that?" I said.

"Yea, sure, let's get on with it," from the lead climber.

I wrote out the note and had all five men sign it. There it was, Lenny France, Northern Alpine Guides. The other men were somewhat hesitant but Lenny overpowered them with his confidence that getting out would be no problem. The climbers grunted their way on past me towards Kennedy with Lenny in the lead, head bowed, and clanking ice axes scaring away the birds.

I continued on another half mile to the upper Kennedy crossing. Like below, it was a mess. The footbridge was gone so it was not an option for a way out. I returned to Kennedy where everyone was settled in around the cabin. It was now five o'clock and no word from Bernie.

"Hello folks, how is everybody doing?" I said.

"Are we going to get out of here tonight?"

"Is there any extra food in the cabin?"

"My wife is really going to be upset if she doesn't hear from me."

The group was getting fidgety. They needed some resolution, a plan.

"Did you see five climbers come down about half an hour ago?"

"Yea, it's the funniest thing. They dropped by here anxious to cross the river and get out. They even asked if anyone wanted to go with them. None of us were interested, so they turned tail and went over near where you came across this morning. Just then, another surge came down the valley and chased them up the hillside. They seemed a little shaken."

"Where are they now?"

"Guess they decided to stick around. They're bivouacked above the washout."

"Kennedy, this is Smith."

The transmission was clear, so Bernie and Jim must be up in the valley somewhere.

"Smith, this is Hanbey. What's your location?"

"We're about halfway up. We're having a little trouble getting around these washouts. We should be near Kennedy in about an hour."

"Everything is stable up here. Be careful when you get near the Kennedy Creek crossing. There are still flood surges coming down and you don't want to meet one personally."

"No problem—we'll check in later," Bernie said.

"What about search and rescue? Are you going to call out the troops?"

"10-4. Before we left, the District Ranger and the County Sheriff's Captain decided to call out Snohomish County Search and Rescue. We met a Deputy Sheriff at the trailhead who said a contingent was on its way up from below. We're also going to officially close the trail to the public."

The group stood listening as I worked my way through this conversation. Normally, I would have gone off alone to use the radio in a situation like this, but it appeared to be reassuring to the group to hear that something was being done. As for me, I needed a moment to take a breather and organize my thoughts.

I hadn't eaten much all day, so I grabbed my grub sack and headed over to the single log bridge that crossed the Whitechuck River, which ran near the cabin. Late afternoon was often a very sweet time at Kennedy. The arch of the sun would sometimes fill the upper Whitechuck valley from the west. The gap formed by the river valley gathered light and made the bridge a serene, dry place. On a typical Cascades day at this elevation, you could get chilled to the bone being outside all day. Direct sunlight was a gift.

I lay back on the log, closed my eyes, and let my thoughts drift off into the sun. It was easy for me to slip off into a daze in the mountains, no matter what the circumstances. I could be hiking along by myself, get drowsy and hole up behind a tree for a nap. I'd wake up and feel perfectly safe and peaceful. All in all, the situation was pretty steady. Everyone else was being very patient. Bernie was headed up, followed by the search and rescue units. I would take a secondary role when they got here. Unfortunately, there was still the matter of the half-buried tent.

I felt good about how I had handled the situation so far. I pulled my boots off and shook debris out from my socks. No matter how well equipped or savvy I tried to be in the back country, my feet always took a beating. I wore nothing but leather boots because of the water and mud. The boots were also a protection from toe stubs and errant tools. Unfortunately, they were extra heavy and didn't allow for much circulation. To pull my wet boots off after a long workday was not a pleasant experience.

As I was airing out my feet and socks, I made some decisions on how to proceed with the group. They needed more specific information on what was going to happen. I owed it to them to let them know that they would probably be spending another night or until the flooding outbursts stopped enough to insure a safe crossing. The area around the cabin had not been flooded but it was dangerously close to the washout. I was nervous about staying on lower ground for the night, but this could be decided a little later. We also needed to organize meals for everyone.

I wandered back over to the cabin and gathered the group.

"It's unlikely that we can get you out safely tonight, but my supervisor is on his way up and will help size things up. Darrington has all of your names and will call your families. I suggest that we set up shop here at the guard station, combine our food, and have a potluck of sorts. I have extra food in the cabin for those who need it. So you know, it's possible that we may need to move up the hillside away from this flood zone for the night, but we'll wait and see."

They were getting tired of this adventure and wanted to go home. The response was accepting but measured. Thankfully, one woman spoke up.

"Let's find out what kind of food we have and organize dinner. We need someone to go for fresh water and something to burn in the woodstove. As long as we're still here, let's make the best of it."

I was more than happy to pass this chore on and defer to her leadership. I had one more unsavory task that I had been avoiding to do before Bernie showed up.

"Listen, I need to check the lower camp area for whatever I can find. I'd like one volunteer to go with me."

In reality, I had been avoiding the prospects of what might await me down in the main camp area, especially under the abandoned tent the people had reported.

I pushed back these thoughts as my conscript and I headed fifty yards downstream. What had been a classic middle elevation back-packing camp replete with several wooden shelters and privies was now in ruin. I'd seen as many as 150 hikers and horsemen camped here at one time. Now, great mounds of glacial till and half buried logs dominated the area. The remaining live trees had gravel and debris mounded 15 to 20 feet up their trunks. It looked like a giant game of pick-up sticks, only some of the sticks were 100 feet long and six feet wide.

"So what are we going to do, look around for missing people?" the volunteer said.

"Well. We're not going to do anything. I'm going in there to see what I can find and you're going up on the hill there. Do you have a whistle?"

"A whistle, what do I need a whistle for?"

"Here, take mine. I want you to watch and listen for any more surges coming down. If you hear or see one coming, blow that whistle like mad."

"Yeah, well, okay, you be careful in there," he said over his shoulder as he headed up the hillside.

I dropped down into the flooded area and immediately stepped into my first sinkhole. I felt a familiar pain shoot up my left leg where I had pulled a muscle the previous summer. I eased my leg out and scraped the muck from my boots. I realized the gravity of my decision to go into the area alone. The rapid action of the torrent repeatedly passing through and receding had left soft spots where the ground hadn't settled.

At first, I couldn't find the tent. I spent 20 minutes doing a cursory check of the area. I saw nothing that gave me a clue. All I could do was look where there had been established campsites. It dawned on me that this is what made this place truly eerie. There was no life there. No birds, ants, animals of any sort. There was nothing green left. The place had suffocated.

My leg was hurting, I was hungry, and I was wandering through a disaster zone alone. I decided to head on back to the cabin and wait for Bernie. Just as I jumped from one log to another, I looked down and saw the tent pole.

A moment of hesitation was all I would give myself, before I dropped down between the logs for a closer look. Yes, it was a tent pole and it was connected to something buried. I grabbed my shovel and began to slowly dig around the aluminum piece, trying not to think about all of the possibilities that could be below.

The pole was buried in sandy muck that had set up to the consistency of soft cement. It was difficult digging. I'd need a pick mattock and rock bar to make any progress here. I left my shovel on the log as a marker and headed back toward the cabin. Just as I waved at my lookout, the radio came alive and startled me.

"Hanbey, this is Smith. You copy?"

"10-4, you must be close, you're coming in loud and clear."

"Well, I think we are too, but I can't get oriented. I assume we're by Kennedy Creek, but it shows Glacier Creek on the map." Bernie's voice echoed over the roar of the river.

"If you were by Kennedy Creek, you'd know it. It's completely bombed out. You come up past Whitechuck Falls yet?"

"Yeah, and that's where we got off track."

"Well, you can try and do what I did. If you're by Glacier Creek, then you need to work your way up to the north side of the washout. Stay in the brush with the flood plain on your right and head due east. After about half a mile you should run into what's left of Kennedy Creek. I suggest you hold up there until it looks like its safe to cross the gorge."

"10-4. We're moving now. I'll check back when we get close."

"Great, good luck."

I decided to return to the buried tent while Bernie and Jim found their way. When I got there, with my volunteer on guard once again, I began to carefully loosen and dig away the debris that entrapped the tent. The rock bar was useful in separating the rocks from gravel, but it was slow work.

I took a moment to think about what lay below. If there was a buried body, Bernie and I would have to carefully excavate it so as not to destroy any tissue. We would have to try and identify who it was then leave them be while the County Coroner came in to verify the cause of death. The body or bodies would undoubtedly be crushed.

I dug my way down past the upper pole and was able to cut away some of the tent material. The whole structure had collapsed in on itself so nothing was revealed. It was time to widen the hole and approach from what appeared to be the shape of the tent.

Things were softening up a bit so I began working with my shovel. I couldn't get away from the vision of penetrating the sand with the point of my fire shovel and piercing an arm or leg or worse. As I continued, it became obvious that this was a small two-person tent. This was gratifying only in that it reduced the possibility of multiple bodies below. I pushed my shovel in a little deeper and felt it give.

I considered waiting for Bernie to proceed, but pressed on hoping to get a little more information. I started easing dirt away with my hands and a small hand trowel. Pretty soon, I could see some color appear. Dark blue. It was heavy material so it could be anything, including clothing. Some more excavation revealed nothing more than a stuff sack. This was a relief.

I pressed on carefully pulling back more debris and more pieces of what once was a typical back country camp. I hauled out a small daypack, candle lamp, writing paper, tennis shoes and a stocking hat—still no body.

"Howdy, you guys looking for me?

I was so shocked by the voice above me that I yelped.

"I don't know, is this your tent?" I said.

"Yeah, I think so—that's my fanny pack.'

I got myself together to ask the obvious.

"Where in hell have you been?"

"I just came down from the climbers camp up on Glacier. Been there all night. What in the world happened here?"

I set back and closed my eyes. Thank God, no tragedy to deal with here. I felt a tremendous burden lifted, like taking a heavy pack off at the end of the day. I gave the young man a quick report on what was happening and took his name as he grabbed what he could of his stuff. I was suddenly feeling exhausted. I needed to get something hot to drink.

I checked in with my lookout, and the three of us went back to the cabin. The sun was dropping and the cabin felt wonderfully warm. I found it a joy to tell the folks the good news about the tent and the overdue climber. I had found nothing. There also hadn't been an outburst from the Kennedy Creek for several hours. Things were calming down.

Bernie radioed just then.

"Hanbey, I'm near the Kennedy crossing. I think we're close."

"Okay, I'll come on down and watch for you."

I settled in on a viewpoint above the creek to wait for Bernie and Jim to crash through the brush somewhere on the other side. I didn't have to wait long.

The orange jacket that Jim used on rescues and during hunting season appeared from behind a stump. I could tell that he and Bernie had been struggling by the way they plopped down to mop their brows.

"What do you want to do?" I radioed across to Bernie.

"Come on over," Bernie said.

"10-4, but you'll have to watch for more flooding down the corridor."

He didn't dawdle. I was surprised at how nimble he was considering his size and the size of his pack. He ambled up to me as if nothing out of the ordinary was going on and dropped his load.

"Pretty dramatic hydraulic event, I'd say."

"So, Bernie, glad you could make it — lose track of yourself back there?" I couldn't help goosing him a bit.

"Not a big deal. Just got disoriented for a minute. Where are the people?"

"Over by the guard station," I said.

"Okay, let's go on over there and figure this thing out."

"I suggest you leave Jim on the other side because he's got a good view up valley in the direction of the surges. You think we'll need him on the other side to coordinate things with search and rescue?"

"Yeah, I'll give him a call."

As we worked our way over to the cabin, I debriefed Bernie on the situation. I could see the climbing group hunkered down on a hillside near where Bernie and I had crossed. It looked like they were going to do what they pleased no matter what the circumstances.

We talked as we walked and agreed that evacuating people down the Whitechuck was the best way to proceed, but not tonight. I also pointed out that the cabin was okay for the time being but that it might not work for the night. When we walked up to the group, I was very relieved to have company in managing this event.

"This is Bernie Smith. He's the Wilderness coordinator for the Darrington Ranger District and we'll be working together to get you out of here."

"Hello everyone, hope you're doing okay. I just came up the Whitechuck trail and it's in pretty bad shape. We're going to figure out a way to get you across the washout safely, and then escort you out to the trailhead," Bernie said.

"Are we here for the night?" One woman asked.

"I can't say for sure, but I think you should prepare yourselves for spending another night. Once, the rescue teams get up here it will be late. No sense trying to negotiate that trail after dark, but we'll see."

Someone offered Bernie a cup of tea and a plate of food as he answered a few more questions.

"Hanbey, this is Jim. You copy?"

"This is Hanbey, go ahead."

"Is everything okay?"

"10-4. Everything is stable over here. You find a place to settle in for the night?"

"No problem, I brought my tent and portable TV. You got an extension cord?"

"Can't help you Jim, the Forest Service didn't pay the power bill and so we've been shut off. Any sign of the troops?"

"Nah, they won't make it up until tomorrow morning, unless they're plain foolish and try to come up what's left of that trail in the dark."

Anything is possible, I thought to myself.

"If they crash into you later tonight, Jim, make sure they don't try and cross the stream."

"10-4. I'll shut the gate. Talk to you in the morning."

"Did you hear from Jim?" Bernie asked.

"Yeah, we just talked and he's set up for the night. He's keeping an eye out for search and rescue."

I sat down while I ate and talked with the solo climber with the buried tent. He described some major rumblings he'd heard coming from the glaciers above the high camp the previous day. He hadn't thought much about it at the time since glaciers were always moaning and groaning. An overload of snow from above and gravity below keep twisting and turning the bowels of these great geologic wonders. I hadn't seen any chunks of ice flowing down with the outbursts over at Kennedy Creek so I really couldn't figure how the glaciers could be involved in this event. No doubt something significant was going on upstream but we could figure that out later.

"So, Bernie, how do you want to handle tomorrow?"

He sipped his tea for a moment.

"I'd say if we go more than eight hours without an outburst, then we could slip these people across on that greasy log. We'll set up a safety line and guide them over. The search and rescue people can take over there and walk them out."

"Sounds good to me. What do you think about settling in here for the night?" I said.

"You know, we can't be sure that another surge off Kennedy Creek might not push its way clear past the cabin. I think we should move uphill for the night."

If safety was our priority, then that made sense. The problem was where to go. All I could suggest, short of hiking the mile back up an established camp at the Cascade Crest Trail junction, was a more or less flat spot two switchbacks up the trail. I laid this out for Bernie and we agreed to present the plan to the group.

"Folks, before the sun drops, we'd like to move this operation up the hill a couple hundred yards. It's just too risky to camp out here on the flats since we can't be sure more flooding might not occur during the night. Plus the weather seems to be holding. Let's grab our gear and get set up before it gets too dark. We can erect a couple of tarps for those of you without tents. Check with Russ if you need extra gear and we'll see what's in the Ranger's Cabin. If the surges have stopped, then first thing in the morning Russ and I are going to drop a tree, set up a safety line and get you across. Any questions or concerns," Bernie said.

The group seemed resigned to another night in the field so everyone mutely shook their heads. We headed out and within 20 minutes were settling into the brushy, but mostly flat spot I'd suggested.

When I finally nestled in for the night, I expected to be wired up from the day. It turned out that I wasn't tucked in more than 30 seconds before the roar of the river lulled me to sleep. The drama wasn't over.

Even though I'd left my radio on, I was too tired to notice that things had gotten exciting down below us. It turned out that 30 search and rescue members had made their way to the Kennedy Creek crossing around 10:30 pm. Jim had been there to slow them down, but their headlamps must have stirred up the group of climbers. Before anyone could say boo, the five climbers came across on the slippery log and asked to be guided out. No sooner had they stepped off the log then another deluge came down the streambed and took everything away. That sobering moment ended the evacuation efforts for the night.

"So what tree do you think will do the trick?" I said.

Bernie had been sizing up several Silver Firs that still stood on our side of the streambed. We'd need one that had enough length to reach over the chasm and the right width to withstand a dead fall without splitting. Bernie's forestry skills came in handy as he was able to pick out what appeared to be a right sized tree for the job.

Since we were in a designated Wilderness area, chain saws were not allowed. Certainly, one could be used in case of an emergency, but the Forest Supervisor would have to approve that. By the time that bureaucratic chain was completed and the saw was brought in, we would be done and taking a nap somewhere. We'd go ahead and drop the tree with the crosscut saw that was kept in the cabin.

I appreciated crosscut saws. They are a highly evolved tool. A well-sharpened crosscut was a joy to use. The cutters and rakes of the blade cleanly spit out fresh curls of clean wood as the tool is pulled from both ends alternately. If two people are working together the task is twice as easy, not half as easy as when the two sawyers are out of sync.

I carried the saw down to the edge of the gorge while Bernie cleared back some room for us to work. He'd picked a fir that was about ninety feet high and three feet across. We'd have to drop the tree at a right angle to the gap in order to match it up with an equally high and flat spot on the other side. Since the flooding had washed away the banks, our tree stood precariously close to the edge. This would put us in a dicey position to operate the saw at just the right angle.

Bernie and I got into position and set to work. We'd radioed to the other side to tell the group to watch their heads. The stranded hikers all hung back 50 yards just in case the tree set out in its own direction

Our first job was to slice about two thirds of the way into the tree on the same side as our fall line. Next, we made a 45-degree cut above the original slice. Then we used an axe to clean out the wood in-between the slice. The resulting divot angled toward our intended direction.

After these cuts, there was just enough wood fiber to hold the tree erect. If the wind came up or the tree was top heavy then it could go over on its own. With an eye toward an escape route, we began a cut with the cross cut on the backside of the tree. Under normal circumstances, a tree will move forward to fill this gap once the supporting tendrils on the backside had been cut. The weight of the tree creates its own momentum and over it goes with a flourish.

This was a pretty minor tree as trees go in the Cascades, but it would take some technique and cooperation to place it where we wanted. At first, one of us pushed while the other pulled, or both of us pulled at the same time or neither one of us pulled at the same speed or rhythm. We were getting nowhere fast and there were a number of interested spectators. We stopped, reset our tempo, and started to make the right kind of progress. The tree began to quiver and lean then gravity took over and down it went with an orchestral crescendo.

After the dust settled, Bernie immediately stepped out on the log and began limbing its topside. I went to work figuring out a way to set up a rigging system to help the people across. I retrieved the climbing ropes, harnesses, webbing, and carabineers that were kept in the cabin in case of climbing mishaps. We never thought that this equipment would be used to usher people across so innocent a place as Kennedy Creek instead of lifting them out of a crevasse up on Glacier Peak.

I tied a rock to one end of a 100-foot nylon cord and tossed the cord across the chasm. Jim and some of the Search and Rescue folks were there to grab the cord on the other side and then slowly pull it in. The other end of the cord was attached to the climbing rope so that it was played out across the gap as the cord was reeled in. Jim cinched the rope to a standing tree on the other side on a line directly above the fallen tree.

I tightened the rope on my side and attached a sling with a carabineer to the guide rope. People could ease their way across the log while holding the climbing rope for support. If they fell, the sling—which would be connected to their waists—would inhibit their fall into the streambed chasm below.

Bernie finished cutting back the largest branches and was working his way back over knocking off stobs so people wouldn't trip. I could see the search and rescue team on the other side positioning themselves to come across.

"Jim, what's going on over there? We don't need those guys over here," I radioed over.

"10-4. I made it clear to them that they can take over when the folks make it to this side. Otherwise, they need to back off."

I was relieved to have Jim on the other bank running interference with the County crews. The trapped people were nervous enough. They didn't need more commotion to raise their anxiety levels.

The group was gathered near me. I explained that they would cross one at a time, and it was up to them whether they wanted to carry their equipment or have it carried across. I would tie each one of them into a harness around their midsection that would then be attached to the guide rope.

"Well, folks, this is it," I said.

"We'll get you over then the search and rescue teams will walk you out. It's been real nice spending this time with you but I'll bet you're a bit antsy to get home."

The group was uneasy. Not only were there people and obligations waiting for them once they got out, but they also had to cross over a torrent on a shaky log to get there.

Bernie and I tied the first person into the harness. Jerry-rigging a support system that would hold the weight of each person would be a challenge. I recalled several stories about climbers who had died when they had fallen and slipped out of their safety harnesses. We were responsible for making sure this didn't happen.

The first person who stepped up on the log was the woman who'd organized the meal last night and helped keep everyone calm. She started to ease her way across after she was clipped in. Bernie had told the group not to look down, just look at the people on either side that were there to help them and keep moving. The woman was very sure-footed and marched across without a hitch. I was relieved not only for the woman but because she set the tone for the rest of the group. Everything was going as planned. I would harness people in, Bernie would check the knots on the harness, and Jim would release them at the other end. The sling material used for the harness and the belay rope was retrieved each time by a pull line.

The last person to make the trip was my volunteer helper. He got half way across and froze. He had been moving too fast and began to lose his balance, so he stopped and wouldn't move forward. We shouted encouragement to him, but it was up to him to compose himself and finish the crossing. Jim stepped up from the other side and began to talk him over. He stayed unruffled which must have helped the guy take the next steps. Soon he was close enough that Jim could offer him a helping hand. Their last step to the other side concluded my end of this episode. We could see the hikers being escorted away in small groups by the rescue teams. It would a tricky and demanding walk out, but they were in good hands.

Bernie and I sat down on a log and watched them trail off into the woods.

"So, Bernie, are you going to stick around and clean up this mess?"

"Nah, now you have something to do this summer. I suggest you make this log walkable. Level it off, then set-up a rope railing if you can. I'd also go ahead and brush out a temporary trail from here to the cabin. We'll get the trail crew up here to start rebuilding the lower trail. Looks like you might be on your own for a while."

I would liked to have had some company for a day or two to talk over this event but it wasn't going to happen.

"Also, get some photos, do an assessment of the damage here and come up with any recommendations you have for setting up new campsites. Jim and I need to head on out with the caravan."

As Bernie worked his way across the log, I stretched out on a rock to have a drink of water. I felt both elated and empty at the same time. I tried to remember if I'd ever been at Kennedy when it was completely empty. No one would be coming up the Whitechuck so it would a lonely place for a while. I laid back, closed my eyes, and took a few deep breaths. I could smell rain in the air.

Start to Finish

SUMMER JOBS WERE HARD TO LAND IN THE SIXTIES. This wasn't due to the lack of work available but to the multitudes of baby boomers coming of age and competing for a finite number of jobs. Unless your dad could get help get you a job with him at local mill, about all that was available in my hometown of Marysville was stoop labor in the local berry fields. I'd work for a month and bring home only $110. And I was a good picker!

With the exception of a government sponsored working trip to Vietnam, the circumstances didn't improve once we graduated high school. A different kind of Federal opportunity that did come along was as a temporary employee with a land management agency. The U.S. Forest Service in particular was not only fully funded by Congress but was flush with timber harvest dollars. This opened the door for a hugely active summer field season. The Mount Baker-Snoqualmie National Forest was no exception and employed hundreds of seasonal workers in timber, fire, trails, recreation, roads, and wilderness within its various Ranger Districts.

Finding outdoor work during that era was a blessing that was both pragmatic and adventurous. For some, laboring in the summer was the meat of their yearly income. Seasonal firefighters often generated enough revenue to hide out in Mexico or Hawaii for the rest of the year. For others, it fit nicely between years in college or as a second income for struggling families. It was a means to an end, yet many walked away with something deeper.

My own outdoor work experience began in 1967 when a friend of a friend helped me nail down a rare opening with the Darrington Ranger District in the North Central Cascade Mountains. I was to be the Green Mountain Fire Lookout. I had no idea what I was getting into, but grabbed the job without hesitation.

I made it through that first summer, and then went on to be a fireguard and a recreation guard. Eventually the opportunity came up to work as a back country ranger in the Glacier Peak Wilderness. I had pined for this type of work for years and snapped up the offer without hesitation. Independently taking on the stewardship of a large chunk of remote landscape required an eclectic mix of skills and experiences and I was up for it. One hour might find you cleaning a back country toilet, the next calling in a fire. One day might be dedicated to hanging a bear line, the next working with a group of volunteers. You might be alone for days or surrounded by dozens of hikers on popular trails. Success required physicality, creativity, and self-reliance.

That initial summer in 1975 as a wilderness ranger was exhilarating. There were seven of us working various remote locations in the Darrington Ranger District that year. Most of my co –workers were in their 20's. They all seemed destined to lead lives of consequence with wilderness work being a cornerstone in their development as adults.

There was Wendy Walker, one of the first women to break the male-only bastion of Forest Service field work. She eventually became an Assistant Professor of Environmental Sciences at Western Washington University. Wendy was smart, opinionated and a lover of all things wilderness. She sported a shock of red hair, a big smile and a quiet strength that helped her look past the institutional barriers that she encountered on the job. Another was Mike Loffler, a Master's level Forest Sciences graduate and climbing guide. Mike was tall, muscular, bearded and a perfect fit for a working life in remote areas. Outgoing and full of life was Sybil Sanford, a highly artistic individual who was finding her bliss in the back country while also breaking the Forest Service gender barrier. Curt Vail was a Fisheries scientist working the high country and lending his quiet wit to all. Rounding out the younger set was Louis Owens, who had a poetic relationship with the back country. He could walk 30 miles a day and later became a professor at several Western universities while gaining notoriety as an expert on John Steinbeck and Native American Literature.

The lead ranger was Ben Englebright. Ben was a retired refinery worker from nearby Anacortes who had started as the first Wilderness Ranger for the District just after the enactment of the Wilderness Act of 1964. He loved to climb mountains and camp for weeks at a time in a platform tent in White Pass with his wife, Lois. In charge of us all was Resource Assistant, Bernie Smith. He knew his stuff and was dedicated to proper Wilderness management. Bernie brought skills as a botanist, photographer and outdoorsman to the table. All in all, I was associated with a high powered group that guided me through my first back country season with both high standards and humor.

The District was massive, embracing 500,000 acres of designated Wilderness and thousands more acres of road-less back country. Much of that that area would later become dedicated Wilderness of its own in 1984. There was no lack of work for anyone. We'd line ourselves up for either daily, five or ten day tours depending on how far back in we were going. After several shakedown cruises with fellow rangers, including an ascent of Glacier Peak, my first assignment was as the Kennedy Ranger. With an old cabin as my home base, I got to rove the western expanses of the Glacier Peak Wilderness. That initial season as a ranger grew into eight more summers and refined my perspective on the whims and vagaries of the job.

For example, the use of the term 'ranger' is a misnomer. There is only one real ranger in a District and that is the District Ranger, otherwise known as the "Big R" ranger. Wilderness or back country rangers are assigned the job title and get to embrace all of the glory, albeit with less responsibility. They also get to wear a patch, name tag and even a badge if there is one lying around the office. Unlike many Forest Service employees, back country rangers actually wear uniforms. The balance of Forest Service workers seem to shun official garb in an attempt to stay out of the cross hairs of an ill-tempered public, but not the Wilderness Rangers with their heightened sense of duty.

Early season trail surveys and clearing is how it all starts on the western slopes of the Cascades. This requires lugging a variety of tools, recordkeeping, and startling the public who actually thought they might have had the trail to themselves. The typical ranger walks local trails until heavy snow takes away any official reason to go on. All the while, they keep track of fallen trees and other major trail problems so they can be managed later on by men and women with even heavier tools. The minor trail problems are ours to preside over as we move along.

Duties include removing any objects on or over the trail, draining away water in an orderly fashion, and picking up last year's garbage. Garbage patrol can get amusing. In the past, I've enjoyed the privilege of jockeying an awful pair of soiled underwear into a garbage bag, removing half a dozen condoms that had been stretched over the butt end of a log, dispatching a maggot infested milk carton, and stripping down entire abandoned campsites. These official duties take away from the main activity of nature study and thinking great thoughts but they do improve the look of things.

Guilt and some kind of undiagnosed complex help fill the ranger's pack with enough emergency gear to solve anybody's moment of misjudgment or recklessness. These items, plus personal gear, a radio, and tools all add up to an oversized burden that defies common sense. Of course, back country worker types embrace this because it's part of our image. No self-respecting wilderness guard goes "lite." We'd rather gut it out with too much in our packs but with our pride intact. This wreaks havoc on unconditioned knees, tweaky backs, and marginal early season stamina. To add to the drama, it's often done in dismal weather.

Most of late spring and early summer in Western Washington is defined by varying shades of grey. Lurking behind the grey blanket are great amounts of moisture that always find a way to release themselves over the foothills and lower slopes of the Cascades. It can start drizzling at the ranger station early morning and continue without hesitation up valley until all are driven out of the woods in a claustro-phobic panic. It can get so dark in the middle of the day under an old growth tree canopy that headlamps are advisable. Cameras default to the flash function and bats begin to prowl in the daytime. No matter the weather, the back country ranger is obligated to be the last one out. It's a shame there's no one around to admire our diligence since everyone has already gone home.

We also have to continually reeducate ourselves on various rules, regulations, policies, and procedures. Being the lone government rep-resentative in remote areas is a heavy burden to shoulder since some of the wildest areas, by their very nature, have some fairly tight guide-lines to protect the resource. Mercifully, we are given the opportunity to interpret them benignly usually faulting on the side of leniency. For example, in the Glacier Peak Wilderness, it is prohibited to "enter or be in a Wilderness with a group exceeding twelve heartbeats." The intent is to keep the number of humans and livestock under control in order to limit impacts. If I took this at face value, I could give a group a hard time if there were twelve of them but one woman was pregnant, thereby adding a hidden heartbeat to the crowd.

Another one of my favorites is a regulation written for the Henry M. Jackson Wilderness that prohibits people from "Camping within 200 feet from the shoreline of Goat Lake." This is just fine, ecologi-cally speaking, but the reality is there are established campsites within that 200-foot range. Trying to camp elsewhere in that lake basin out-side of 200 feet would require folks to attach themselves to almost vertical walls. The fun for the back country ranger is asking people im-properly camped to move within the boundaries, especially on a cold day when the offenders are already hunkered down in their tent. This is where I'm thankful for Regulation 36CRR261.10(d) that prohibits the "discharge of firearms within 150 yards of a developed and/or oc-cupied area." I can always pull that one out of the hat if the scofflaws draw a bead on me with one of several weapons.

Getting equipped at the start of the season is also entertaining. The cache of outdoor equipment is often well worn and dated. The packs and raingear are especially ripe carrying the odor of many sweaty trips and long-term storage in an unvented attic. You don't really discover the zippers that stick or the gnawed mouse hole until a trip or two into the season. To be honest, most self-respecting rangers would probably reject a newly minted pack for one with character and credibility.

Ultimately, back country rangers are supposed to be the hippest ones in the woods. We know all and see all. Wrong. There are Cub Scouts with sharper equipment than we have and know how to use it. I even got jealous of their uniforms on occasion. Additionally, the 21st Century version of the little tykes have GPS and satellite driven cell phones strapped to their little belts with mom on speed dial. I carried a radio that only works when you don't really need it. Any obstacle, such as a large tree, nullifies its effectiveness. It's reassuring to have, though. You can always crawl to within radio range after losing a finger to an errant axe swing. Or find a Cub Scout.

Such is the work of the Wilderness Ranger. It can be noble and uninspired, rhapsodic and mundane. Most often, the only audience is a crow perched on a nearby tree acknowledging the ranger's work with a chuckle or a scoff.

Handmade cedar chair, Kennedy Hot Springs cabin, Glacier Peak Wilderness July, 1975. Photo by Bernie Smith

Young man exercising a horse just off shore on the Dingle Peninsula, Ireland July, 2007. Photo by Jeanne Anderson.

OTHER

BACKDROPS

Parallel Journeys

THE GRIZZLY SIDLED ACROSS THE BACKDROP of the cliffy stream edge as we gathered our gear and moved slowly in the opposite direction. We did as we had been told and lumped ourselves together so we might appear larger as a group. We didn't panic as the bear turned to face us, his thick head and broad shoulders swaying slightly as he sized us up. We were thirty feet apart and eyeballing each other with measured deference. The drama seemed to play itself out in slow motion. As we eased our way upstream, the bear sniffed the air then moved on in the opposite direction.

The bear had come foraging along the stream as we dozed after lunch from a long morning of wet and cold stream restoration work along Moose Creek in the Alaska interior. Cynthia, one of the high school students on our Student Conservation Association crew, had awoken first. In her surprise, she had yelled, "Lion!"

We gathered our stuff and sidled off in one direction while the bear moved the opposite way. Once safely away, we sighed collectively and organized ourselves for the afternoon's work. This was another potent adventure to add to a growing repertoire that would add up to a powerful summer for all of us. What we didn't know was that thirty miles to the northeast of us and just outside the Park boundary was another young man, not much older than our crewmembers who was slowly starving to death. It would be another two months before the world learned of Chris McCandless and his chosen fate.

My wife, Jeanne, and I were leading a crew of six teenagers in Denali National Park during the summer of 1992. We were recruited and trained by the Student Conservation Association, an organization with a long history of providing volunteer work crews of youth and young adults for our national parks and forests. Our initial job was to implement a streamside rehabilitation project orchestrated by Denali Park engineers. Later, we would be helicoptered to the base of Mt. McKinley and work on restoring old road ruts that led to an abandoned airfield that had been built before the establishment of the existing six million acre park in 1980.

Our six teenage participants had come from all over the country with the lure of Alaska in their blood. There was Cynthia, fresh from her private school in Maine, full of life and ready to take on anything wild and free. John was from Kansas and grown up on a farm. He wore his brother's army fatigues, and was anxious to spot wildlife with a hunter's eye. Sarah was from New York and was primed up for a powerful group experience, no matter where it was. Bigger than life and full of fun was Liam, the son of a Pittsburgh steel worker. The third female was Laura, hesitant and withdrawn but game for whatever lay ahead. Finally, there was Brinton. He was from Seattle and was easily prepared for anything that might confront him in the wilds of Alaska.

Like McCandless, our crew was looking northward with stars in their eyes. They had no illusions about living off the land but they knew that anything "Alaska" was going to be bigger than life. Even at their young age, the Last Frontier State had entered their consciousness as a raw and wild landscape, remotely connected to the U.S. proper. Just like Chris McCandless, they seemed to know that time spent in the back country of Alaska would be a defining moment in their lives.

As we gathered our crew in Anchorage and made final preparations for four weeks of work in Denali, Chris McCandless (later immortalized in John Krakauer's bestseller *Into the Wild*) had already worked his way into the Alaska wilderness west of Healy. He had crossed the Teklanika River at low water and found an abandoned bus to inhabit while he continued his personal journey of seclusion and self-discovery. He lived there for four months before succumbing to starvation and possible toxic poisoning from some plants he had eaten out of desperation.

Our crew would live in similar environmental conditions as McCandless. The landscape, weather, remoteness, and presence of predatory animals were all the same. Our group was younger than McCandless yet were willing to take similar risks and measure themselves against the elements. The primary difference was our crew were prepared and supported by caring adults.

While McCandless slept in an abandoned bus, our crew slept on the ground. They also worked all day in either bone chilling weather or mosquito saturated heat and shared the landscape with large four-legged carnivores. We carried no weapons, using only learned knowledge of how to manage ourselves around wild animals. This was tested as our crew interacted with grizzlies on two occasions at close range and came away unscathed. This included an intimate experience with a sow and cubs and the aforementioned streamside standoff that ended benignly.

Our perspective was one of safety and common sense, not the naïve strategy of McCandless. Our experience didn't dissolve into a life and death struggle, yet we were in a position where Mother Nature could have taken charge. For example, our forty-mile cross-country recreation hike at the end of our assigned work weeks required crossing three rivers, including the mile wide McKinley Bar. We selected an early morning crossing, recognizing the wisdom of not challenging the river after a day of snow melt off nearby Mt. McKinley. We traversed from sand bar to sand bar with our arms interlocked and facing upstream. We wore neoprene socks, which cut the frigid cold of the glacier melt water.

We emerged chilled but elated and continued on to a bus awaiting us at Wonder Lake.

McCandless did try to leave his hermitage but was pushed back by the Teklanika River. This forced him back into his shell and, ultimately, his death. The river had risen over its banks as a result of a

25-year rain event and blocked his pathway out. We encountered the same flooding along our creek. The deluge washed many of our tools away but our work held up.

Chris McCandless also cast fate to the wind by not having an adequate map of the area, which would have offered him several alternatives. We carried a detailed map and were able to easily navigate ourselves over miles of road-less and trail-free terrain, choked with muskeg, willow thickets, and a somewhat featureless landscape.

Our strength was in our preparation, confidence, and ability to adapt. Our experience was not destined to be tragic. We didn't underestimate the powerful personality of the Alaska outback. No one will make a feature-length film of our journey. Instead, we all came away with intrinsic measures of growth and an optimistic relationship with wilderness.

Walking the Dingle Way

FROM A DISTANCE, IT LOOKED LIKE A LARGE DOG moving slowly into the sea with something white and fleshy clinging to its back. Another ten minutes of walking brought things into focus. On this quiet and remote beach near the western edge of Ireland was a young man exercising a horse in neck deep water. Riding bareback and almost naked, the lad was nurturing the steed through a briny watercourse. The animal seemed none too happy about the arrangement and soon prevailed over its trainer and made its way back to the beach. It was raining and fifty degrees but the young man was undaunted as he clambered atop another waiting horse and headed back in. Moments later, when my wife Jeanne and I stopped gawking and walked on, several thoroughbreds with their costumed jockeys bore down on us in full stride. We thought we were walking on an isolated beach but instead seemed to have stumbled onto an informal racetrack. We stepped aside as the horses galloped by, noses flaring, foamy expectorant flying everywhere, leaving us with the feeling of excited invisibility. This was quintessential Ireland—down to earth, tactile, and full of life.

In the summer of 2007, my wife Jeanne and I were day four into a hundred plus mile walk around the Dingle Peninsula in southwest Ireland and the unexpected and entertaining were becoming the norm. Our ten-day self-guided hike was leading to the discovery of a rich culture with its feet firmly in the past and its head in the future.

The Dingle Peninsula lies on the southwest corner of Ireland, a five-hour train ride back in time from Dublin. This relatively small appendage of land houses a high concentration of all that is "Ireland." While it's easy to get distracted by the verdant backdrop as you walk, occasional stone pillars remind you that you are, indeed, on the Dingle Way Walking Trail, the route of an ancient religious journey.

In one day of walking, you might follow aged rock walls high above villages, cross several streams, then drop down to a boulder strewn beach. Another day might take you on main roads and through "green paths," pastures, and backyards. It all adds up to a 111-mile constitutional that circumnavigates the whole peninsula and immerses the hiker in a wide range of scenery and experiences. Much of the route is along an ancient pilgrimage route, though today the more remote parts are the domain of sheep and occasional herds of milking cows.

No one day was the same as the next. Our printed guide for day seven stated that we'd "experience an exciting day's walk to a saddle on the Brandon Mountain range, then drop down, enjoying spectacular views along the way, to the shore of Brandon Bay." In contrast to that optimistic description, we stood at the saddle of Brandon Mountain in the driving rain, boggy glop underfoot, able to only see ten feet in front of us.

Nearby was a 2,000-year-old Ogham stone which let us know we were at the pass since we couldn't really tell up from down. Ogham monuments are found throughout Ireland and carry the mysteries of an ancient alphabet and messaging system. Hidden off in the mist was a "ring fort" that housed underground chambers thought to be the dwelling place of fairies. Further out in the distance was the eerie bleating of a lone, seemingly lost sheep. This four-legged foghorn was somewhat reassuring despite the sketchy pathway before us that dropped into a fog bank.

Earlier that day, we'd marched up this typical sheep path. Over our shoulder were the Blasket Islands, the closest point in Europe to North America. The route required us to tiptoe through boggy fens and over random watercourses. On higher ground, the pathway became the domain of resident flocks of sheep where their droppings pointed the way upward. The whole show reminded us of the mountainous terrain around our hometown of Seattle, where clouds can drop rapidly leaving the wanderer disoriented.

No matter where we went, Ireland embraced us with a wink and a smile. Home of the Celtic Tiger, the namesake for their economic boom of the previous ten years, Ireland was open and ready for business. Here was a country that exported half of its population 160 years before due to famine and despair, only to celebrate the lowest unemployment rate in Europe in the here and now. As with America, much of their menial labor was now the domain of the immigrant, in this case Polish, Lithuanian, Nigerian, and Chinese workers. Here is the land of Irish football, soccer, rugby, horse racing, cricket, and a particularly ferocious sport called hurling. Hurling is where two teams carry clubs and batter each other and a ball about until time runs out or the last man is standing. The Irish are such sports fans that easily half of their many daily papers seemed to be given over to fact and opinion about the world of Irish sport.

In contrast to our sober walkabout, Ireland's quirky press was also dedicating a lot of ink amusing their readers with the story of a young fellow from Australia who was traversing Ireland south to north. He was stopping at every pub along the way for a pint to raise money for charity. He insisted on calling his trek a "fund raiser" and started out carrying a stuffed donkey called Asal. Unfortunately, his mascot was purloined half way through and there was a uniquely Irish outcry in response. Three days later, the Irish Independent newspaper carried this headline: "Nameless Woman Saves Pub Crawl Aussie's Precious Ass." Not only was this representative of the creative writing that saturated the Irish press, but it also put the man back on track and allowed him to complete his journey of 254 pints of Guinness.

Our walk occurred during the wettest weather in 200 years. Quaint byways became suck holes of cow manure, sheep goop, and puddles. To step off trail anywhere would lead to either dense hedgerows, or impassable bogs of heather and gorse. Another alternative was a nearby road, often the private raceway for mostly impatient drivers, none of whom understood the value of international relations and our personal safety. No matter, the tradeoffs were worth it.

The Dingle Way wasn't really a trail but a track that connected village and farm, beach and mountain, pub to pub. On any given day, we'd emerge from our lodging to follow a series of posts signifying the right way to go on the Dingle Way. We'd sidestep cars, animal leavings, and squalls as we completed ten to eighteen miles per day. We'd follow centuries old rock walls, overhanging corridors of fuchsia, wild rose and buddleia, shorelines, cobbled walkways, and even a gravel road or two. All paths led to a bed and breakfast or a pub, a place to eat nearby. Each one was different from the next and represented the large variety of the tourist accommodations available on otherwise bucolic stretches of land.

On one rainy day, we stumbled upon the western most golf course in Europe, called Ceann Sibeal. This "links" course was so remote and exposed that it had a windsock mid-course to let golfers know the direction of the near constant wind. Another day, we wandered into a seaside pub that served up two pieces of white bread married by a slice of ham and mustard and called a sandwich. Of greater interest were the locals in rubber boots and wool hats topping off their third or fourth pint of the day. This was indicative of Irish social life (one town had 108 residents and nine pubs) but not Irish cooking.

We had expected mutton and Irish stew and not the quality seafood, pasta, cheeses, and desserts that were lovingly served in almost every small restaurant we visited. Accompanying these meals, including breakfast, was the Irish obsession with corny American music. It was everywhere. One fine meal in an ancient restaurant was marred by a repeating loop of Carpenter songs. We had expected rich and wonderful Irish music everywhere but had to settle for Tom Jones and Frank Sinatra. We did attend a concert in an old church in Dingle that featured an ancient Irish bagpipe called the Uilleann, but had to go out of our way to find this. This did not make sense to us, but did add to our impression of Ireland as a land of contrasts.

Near the end of our walk was a geological wonder: the Magharees Peninsula. Connected to the mainland only by sand dunes, this *tom bolo* (headland) made for fine walking. On the west side were five miles of the North Atlantic. In between lay a hidden fishing village on picture perfect Scaggane Bay, with the final miles along the rocky beaches of Tralee Bay. In between, we once again ran into horses wandering the beach from one pasture to another giving us no more than a wink and a nod.

The hard edge of historical Irish life was seen daily in the rock constructs used by early pilgrims, sheepherders, and soldiers. One day we passed the Dun an Oir (Fort of Gold) where over 700 Spaniards had been captured and beheaded by the English in 1580. Later, we stumbled upon a beautiful rock structure called the Giffany Bridge. In the same year, 1580, English Lord Grey had marched his men over this bridge and headed for Smerwick Harbor where he executed 600 captive men, women, and children. Even our last day was filled with the historical exploits of Cromwellian soldiers where the population of a Magharee village was "blown up to powder" while hiding in the Minard castle nearby.

Ah the Irish! No wonder doom and gloom and the magical world of guilt prevails. Almost daily, we'd see written and public affirmations of their suffering. "Steal a buoy, steal a life" was the script attached to life buoys along the shore. "Pay the fare or pay the price" showed as a warning for scofflaws in the trams of Dublin. Even on the beach at the popular seaside resort of Inch was posted, "Farewell dear Inch, As I must Leave, As I have promises to keep before my last sleep."

We wound down our walk where we began, in the town of Tralee. Here was where old and new Ireland seemed to collide with traditional streets, churches, and gardens facing chain stores and traffic jams. We did discover their stunning rose gardens and enjoyed two inebriated duffers sitting on a bench harmonizing over the classic "Rose of Tralee," their voices mingling with the mist in ephemeral Ireland.

Glacier Peak from the west, North Central Cascades

ARTICLES

20 Loads

THE MOON WAS JUST EMERGING FROM ITS ELLIPSE on this August morning as we gathered around the shop area of Sahale Construction along Lake Union in Seattle. It was still dark, but the crew was going about its work with quiet efficiency, readying themselves for a long day in the mountains. We piled into the oversized rig and headed out.

Blending in with early morning traffic and the rough edges of Mercer Avenue, it was hard to believe that the five men in this truck/ trailer would find their way to the exposed and icy slopes of Mt. Rainier, some 100 miles away and 10,000 feet higher. Instead of down coats and climbing boots, this crew was equipped with Carharts and work boots. No need for ice axe and crampons, when shackles, tie downs and cargo nets were needed. Working man's hard hats would be required, not climbing helmets. The job for this 14 hour day was to top off a three year reconstruction job at Camp Muir, high camp for the southern climbing routes on Mt. Rainier. The day was full of promise, only slightly tinted by the specter of impending hazardous and hard work.

Camp Muir, way station over the decades for thousands, had gotten itself a face lift. Several years of planning and months of on-the-ground work had delivered significant improvements to this rag-tag village in the sky. Instead of the noisy, messy, dank hovels that served as the public shelter, cook shack and privy, newly rebuilt structures had revitalized those spaces with rustic allure and stability.

Camp Muir has housed the adventurous and the scientific for 86 years. It is strategically placed at 10,000 feet, some 4,600 feet above Paradise Lodge yet 4,000 feet below the summit. Named after celebrated wilderness sage John Muir, this narrow ridgeline between the Nisqually and Cowlitz Glaciers provides a sanctuary for the weary on stable ground, despite being fully exposed to the elements.

The Guide Shelter was built in 1916 and is the oldest rock structure in the Park. 1921 brought the construction of the Public Shelter, then the erection of the toilet by CCC workers in1936. All were failing and in dire need of reconstruction. Along came Ellen Gage and her crew of historians at the Park. Meetings were held, planning took place and eventually Sahale Construction won the bid for the high elevation work project.

As the truck bounced its way down past Tacoma and on through the endless strip of neon and traffic lights that defines Spanaway and Parkland, the sun began to lighten the sky. The early morning chatter of working people picks up. Behind the wheel is Aaron Nelson, young, confident and seemingly ready to take on the day. Filling up the back seat are Steve Howell, Marty Walz and Keith Jellerson. Steve and Brian are regular employees of Sahale, but Keith, who runs his own business, is just along for the day.

Seated in the middle front is Carroll Vogel. Carroll is the Principal Manager, team guidance counselor and quiet inspiration behind the bridges, trails and special back country projects that Sahale has designed, fabricated and erected in difficult landscapes throughout the country. As with most people who manage complex projects, I expect his mind is preoccupied with the many details and arrangements that have to fall into place to make this day a success. Or maybe he is replaying the previous night's loss to the Angels or thinking about his kids.

The road winds its way out of suburban sprawl into more scenic farmsteads and intersection businesses. The trees get taller and more tightly packed and soon we are approaching the gateway cities to Mt. Rainier National Park. These small towns seem relatively prosperous despite the dramatic flooding that had closed down the Park for an historic period of time just months previously.

Along the way, we get an occasional glimpse of THE MOUNTAIN, which is cloud free and glistening. Though unspoken, the work crew appears to be elevated by this sight, since bad weather in mountainous terrain makes for a very long workday. This is building to be a pristine work day in spectacular terrain, coming near the end of a long, wet summer that is almost history.

Adding to the buzz in the cab is the upcoming opportunity to spend the day working with Anthony Reese, legendary Cascade Mountain helicopter pilot. Tony is 71, in recovery from his first serious crash in 30 years of flying last spring, and the only person that Carroll and his crew trust to fly the tricky slopes of Mt. Rainier. Multiple trips loaded with both humans and unwieldy cargo are involved and no one wants to toss the dice on a pilot they didn't know. Tony has a reputation with all of the regional National Forests and Parks as the person of choice for smaller, complicated lifts and deliveries in and around the remote traces of the Cascades and Olympics.

The truck rounds a bend and pulls into Ricksecker Point, a closed off viewpoint several miles below Paradise. Directly in front of us is the expansive west face of Mt. Rainier which starts low and continues upward over tier after dramatic tier until the summit snowfield of Rainier trails off into the heavens. Our destination for the day is up and out of sight to the southeast over Mazama Ridge and atop the Muir snowfield.

We are greeted by a man dressed in a flight helmet, orange jumpsuit and expansive smile. Rich Lietner is the Park Service 'ground man' for the day for their share of loads being flown back and forth to Camp Muir. Rich is a man of multiple talents, on the one hand having earned a Doctorate and on the other making himself an expert on high elevation toilets. Some of the Park's earlier loads that day have been sealed barrels of semi-decomposed human waste. Camp Muir and the higher camp on Ingraham Flats produce a monumental amount of excrement, much of which, in previous years, worked its toxic way into down glacier watersheds. Now, most of it is collected and hauled offsite, paid for, in part, by the $40.00 climbing permit required to ascend Rainier.

Rich is the perfect person for the job. Highly competent, broadly educated, he is a jack-of-all mountain trades sort of Park Service seasonal employee. He is the kind of person that the current administration felt compelled to eliminate and replace with task specific contractors several years previous. An outcry from Park Administrators and worker organizations thankfully nipped that in the bud before a bad idea became reality.

Pretty soon, the drone of a small helicopter increases in intensity, and approaching, off to the east, is our workhorse for the day. The four passenger Hughes 500 helicopter swoops in over the parking lot from on high, gently lays down another barrel, and flies off for its last load for the Park. Carroll's crew holds back until the humming of the engine fades then starts setting up for their end of the work day. The plan is for Carroll, Eric, Keith and I to fly up to Muir for the day and package up the loads of left-over construction debris, leaving Brian and Steve at the parking lot to manage things as they are dropped off.

Back comes Tony 15 minutes later and gingerly sets the helicopter down as if it were a leaf off a tree in late fall. He approaches the waiting group with the type of confidence mixed with humility that people of substance exude later in life. Carroll stops the proceedings and presents Tony with a dedicated photograph acknowledging their work from the summer before. Neither man knows quite what to say, but the measured deference and affection between the two men is obvious. Since no politicians are present, the formalities are over in short order—it's time to get down to the business at hand.

Tony gathers us all together and talks about the conventions and safety needs we'll all have to honor when working around the machine. He semi-jokingly tells the group to treat the helicopter 'as if it were trying to kill you.' This means to assume nothing, follow established protocols and don't be stupid. Once said, he loads up our first human occupants and prepares to disembark. One of his biggest concerns is flying the chopper in tight spaces and thin air around Camp Muir, where there are dozens of people already gathered for their trips up and down Mt. Rainier. We'll have to work with care and efficiency to set-up our loads safely since most of them will not be taken from the helipad but from around the reconstruction sites and groupings of people.

Depending on the helicopter's level of fuel, we'll have to gauge the size of our loads to about 500 pounds a carry. Each load will have to be netted up with a swivel clamp on top so that Tony can electronically release them at the parking lot below. The hazards for the pilot, and for all of us for that matter, are not only the lean air that reduces the effectiveness of the rotor blades, but unpredictable updrafts and downdrafts, intensely reflected sun off the glaciers, and ungainly loads that might throw the helicopter off balance. An extra added attraction will be rotor wash from the hovering helicopter which will kick up plumes of volcanic pumice and anything else not tied down.

Within an hour, Tony begins sweeping loads off the mountain. Each trip is called a 'turn' and represents a round trip. Each load is different enough that aerobatics and finesse are vital on each turn. Radio communications and hand signals keep all parties connected but in the end it is the skill of the pilot that kept the process safely flowing.

To our advantage on this day is the friendly weather at Camp Muir. It is mostly calm and surprisingly balmy. The views off in every direction are amplified by residual moisture in the air. Camp Muir itself is alive with climbing groups and guides, day hikers, Park service workers and us. In contrast, we are surrounded by absolute quiet punctuated only by the roar of the Hughes sweeping in and out every 20 minutes or so and the 'Mountain' itself delivering occasional salvos of rock and ice fall.

The reconstruction of three of the primary buildings at Muir is inspired. The exteriors have been rebuilt to reflect the design and look of the original buildings. Rock extrusions along the rooflines called crenellations mimic the sharp rock outcropping nearby. The exterior of each building is dressed in locally collected rock and just below roof line are cantilevered timbers that act as roof joists on the interior and ornamentation on the outside. The interiors of each building have been efficiently redesigned to maximize space, storage and insulation needs. Door frames have been moved to face warmer southern exposure and are adorned with attractive and practical iron mongery. Even tubular sky lights have been installed to lighten interiors and concrete spread on the roofs for durability and water proofing.

One trip leads to another until it is time for Tony to gas up. We fuel ourselves with lunch and enjoy the sustained silence for a while. Off on the horizon are Mt. Adams, Mt. Hood, and Mt. St. Helens puffing away. All of the ridgelines and watersheds that connect them are distinct on this clear day. Over our shoulder are groups of climbers snaking their way up and down the hillside, their routes clearly defined in the snowfields. We lay back as silent observers, enjoying the show.

After freighting down 20 loads and 10,000 lbs. of debris, the work day is drawing nigh. As we pull away, we are encouraged by the now more natural and uncluttered look of the place. This, of course, will be taken for granted by subsequent legions of visitors to Muir. This is as should be—come in, do the job, and leave no trace. For us, the flight down is as dreamy as this world of ice and snow. We buckle everything down and head out for our head bobbing, joke filled commute back to the city.

This Article originally appeared in the October 28th, 2008 edition of *Washington Trails Magazine* entitled "Rebuilding Camp Muir: Restoring the historic shelters at the base camp for Mt. Rainier."

Black Mountain High Route

When 5:00 am rolled around, Bill and I were primed and ready to go. A combination of eagerness, anxiety, and expectancy permeated our thoughts as we prepared for a day in the high country of the Cascade Mountains. Today would be filled with freelance roaming along the Black Mountain High Route, a unique and remote off-trail track on the Southwest flanks of Glacier Peak. It wasn't all play. The route was a shortcut to the Pacific Crest Trail, where, as a back country ranger for the Forest Service in 1975, it was my responsibility to manage.

We ate rapidly, filled out packs with equipment necessary to cross a variety of terrain, and poked our heads outside of the ranger's cabin at Kennedy Hot Springs for a peak at the weather. As with most of August this year, a grey mass hovered overhead. Fortunately, it appeared to be around 7,000 feet and rising, so we agreed to give it a try. I had seen the area we were headed for, but had never been through it. From any angle, it was fascinating country. Rarely traveled by anyone, we expected it to be private and primeval.

The westerly section of the route begins with an unpleasant climb up 49 switchbacks on what is identified as a "no-nonsense" trail. An elevation gain of 2,900 feet in two and a half miles took us from valley bottom to tree line in a hurry. The trail, which eventually deposits plucky hikers at Lake Byrne, was built in the 1930s under the tutelage of then District Ranger, Harold Engles. Apparently, when those working on projects in the Kennedy Hot Springs area below wanted to fish Lake Byrne above, they would follow the trace of a mountain goat path from the salt-saturated hot springs up to the lake. Later, when a trail was proposed, it was built along this tract, which was the shortest distance from the bottom to the top.

It was a rude way to start the day. Tight, slowly churning muscles made the lake a joyful relief to see. It represented the end of a forty-nine act bad dream and a true commitment to the route—a departure from the security of the trail to the exotic appeal of the unknown. Mind and body were stimulated as we geared up to move beyond Lake Byrne. Bill didn't say much. His thoughts were evident by his smile.

We picked our way up through snow and boulders to a U-shaped col that connects two prominent pinnacles at the east end of the lake. From this point we traversed a long sloping grade that forms the western extremities of Black Mountain. We followed a faint goat trail to the ridge top with terraced snowfields stretching for miles to our left and rock buttresses to our right. A family of grouse let us nearly walk over them before retreating in a flurry uphill. I felt like I was trespassing on posted land.

Upon reaching the ridge top, we were greeted with a view of the secluded headwaters of Lost Creek. Before us was a genuine hidden valley that would take hours to bushwhack across if we got off route, but we intended to pass above the head of this vast chasm without too much concern. Other emotions were welling up. Moving beyond this ridge top represented independence and isolation. Decisions would be crucial. Self-reliance would be on trial. Who would take care of Bill's cat if we never came back?

Even though Black Mountain was in the clouds, we could see where we wanted to go. The question of how to get there would be something else. We choose to head downward at an angle rather than following the ridge we were on. We soon realized this was a mistake. We dropped down and around several bluffs we had not seen from above, but we were losing altitude even though progressing toward our objective. We were navigating through a giant maze with false walls and dead ends. The security of each open patch of grass would soon be enveloped by subalpine firs and steep rock. Finally we committed ourselves to the least imposing cliff and carefully worked our way down into a large plateau below. We were rewarded with an open, pristine basin laced with polished boulders, melt ponds and views upward toward the stark flanks of Black Mountain.

It was a lot of effort expended in order to find a secluded place to eat, but the water features and rock gardens justified any qualms. We settled back for some goodies and a moment of reflection on our next move. The overcast had turned to light mist and fog which was obscuring our view toward a key pass that we needed to find to skirt the southern bulk of Black Mountain.

We needed a wider and clearer view of the situation, so we climbed up into a small notch in the rock ridge directly in our path. From this point we could now see our objective. We could also see that we would be involved in a long sweeping uphill traverse on a precipitous southern slope. Long stretches of snow, some of it exposed and passing over water channels, occurred at frequent intervals along the way. The next hour of scrambling was filled with an erratic mixture of rubble gullies, rock faces, loose scree, heather slopes and generally steep terrain. The gradient was continually to our left, so when we arrived at the melt line just below our hoped-for access to Black Mountain, our legs were wobbly at best. We stopped for a break and a glance upward.

Intuition was to be our guide for the climb up the southern buttress. Lines on a topographic map do not address themselves to the push of the facial features of the land. Logic and common sense tell you to take the lines of least resistance up through unknown realms. Instinct takes you beyond that. It collates past experiences and knowledge buried in the subconscious into an almost impulsive feeling of what lies beyond the view. Our grasp of the situation told us to move upwards and to the right, bisecting the natural contours of the land.

I took the lead here as we climbed over moderately steep snow and occasional patches of rock. The mountain was surreal. Mist was flowing down the slope. It was uniquely quiet, but at the same time almost hissing in an eerie loneliness. We continued to climb unroped, as the snow was firm and there were good run outs below. The rock portions were smooth to the touch and covered with adequate holds and predictable routes. They were also valuable because they allowed us to skirt areas of vertical and questionable snow. I fell once, but the bite of my ice ax was abruptly efficient.

After 1,000 feet of climbing, things began to level off and we experienced our first pure patch of alpine flowers. Against the surrounding snowfields, they protruded with a pastel blue delicacy. First accents and daredevil dramatics are not why I come to the mountains. Sights such as these are the drawing card. The pass could now be seen above us, so we scrambled up and over. A whole new vista greeted us. More peaks, valleys, moving water and melt ponds. It was also time for lunch.

Food and fluids were important, but we also needed to let the adrenalin of the completed ascent subside. We mixed a bottle of lemonade, cut cheese and salami, and ate our way through an indulgent half hour. Soon it was pushing 1:00 pm and we had much more ground to travel.

Our next move involved a descent of five or six hundred feet to a terrace below. I cleverly led us into a tight spot over a sharply steep rock gulley. Descending this slope was a strain due to loose rock and a bit of tension between Bill and me. This predicament was my doing and Bill is not a vindictive person so chose to not trundle any rocks in my direction. At the bottom we saw our first deer, exchanged glances and took off in our own direction. Ours was to the Northwest and gradually uphill towards Skullcap Peak.

We entered a truly magnificent world of color, smells and filtered light. It was hard to stay on track with all the distractions. A pinnacled landmark indicated that we were now on the northwestern side of Skullcap. Here, a semi-circular bowl of rock and snow defined the landscape. We decided to edge our way across the top of this amphitheater, then glissade down to the bottom in order to stay on route. Skullcap Peak was not visible to us, so we simply went straight up towards a predetermined point.

We passed water falling over slick rock and ice, huge boulders and debris from the eroded peaks above. At the base of these ragged fingers of rock, we navigated to the right and after having ruffled a gathering of marmots, found ourselves overlooking the southeast side of the mountain. We could now see the lower slopes of Glacier Peak, the upper Whitechuck River drainage and our eventual high route destination, Red Pass. We could also see a lot of walking and two more peaks to cross.

The next section was the most risky of the trip. We dropped down over terraced cliffs, clinging patches of heather, talus slopes and more snow. The decisive hazard though, was the exhaustion creeping into our mental and physical equipment. Our movements were slow and orderly, but nothing could reduce an edge of apprehension in our attitudes. The few patches of snow were icy and steep, so we roped across them carefully. Well-rooted plants were the only things that kept us from peeling off the slope on several occasions, but we kept on until we attained a safe point on an ascending ridge leading to the next peak.

Though continually up and down, this section was classic ridge top walking. Sloped steeply on both sides, but with a well-defined walkway in between, the way renewed our spirits and self-assurance. We had walked our way through seven miles of continual up and down with constant stress on legs, knees and ankles. Now it was time to relax on a moderately steep grade to the next rolling summit.

Acres of wildflowers surrounded us so we literally tiptoed through this garden. We strolled alone, consumed by our own diversions. The violently beautiful east slope of Sloan Peak was over my right shoulder. Vast snowfields and talus slopes leading to an occasional small lake dominated the scene below. After an unexpected and exposed scramble, I crept to within easy reach of the next summit. Bill had dropped back to avoid my rock fall so I was soon alone atop this 6910 foot unnamed peak. Several items captured my attention. The crest of this fine young mountain was blessed with orange peels and a fire ring.

We had spent ten hours alone in an area totally devoid of any trace of humanity, but seeing these symbols of civilization was like fishing an isolated alpine lake and snagging a tuna fish can. I was not surprised or particularly dismayed. I was simply reminded that true isolation from my species is nearly impossible. Many people I've met in the back country seem to function best with things of familiarity around them. Equipment, trails, shelters, toilets and the like seem to keep things in perspective for us all. We lean on each other for security even while seeking solitude.

We were near the end of the route and its terminal, the Pacific Crest Trail, but we were several hours behind schedule. Ten miles remained on our loop back to Kennedy Hot Springs and I had to pick up garbage, check toilets and fire rings and the like, all before dark. We did what repairs we could to this marvelous viewpoint and set our sights for 7,000-foot Portal Peak.

Bill led for the next hour up through steep meadow and brush to this last summit. The top provided a fitting climax for our efforts. A crazy quilt of glaciers, meadows, streams, jagged peaks and other delights that defined the southern flanks of Glacier Peak were laid before our eyes. The clouds had opened to shower sun on our backs and a warm wind stroked our faces. We were satiated with the physical and sensual intensity of the whole experience. It was time to go home.

The trip back was a blur. There're not usually many people moving around at dusk in the high country, so we had the remaining eight miles of trail to ourselves. I was surprised when we emerged from the twilight to talk with campers at their campsites. We must have looked like some sort of governmental apparition skulking around in the shadows. More than one roach or bottle of wine was quickly hidden as we passed by.

The last stretch back to the cabin was completed in the darkness and moon shadows. We had a contest going to see who could stumble over the most stobs and roots, but it didn't matter since we were numb by now.

Finally, after sixteen hours and seventeen miles on an alpine roller coaster, we returned full circle to my cabin. Food in great volumes was our first priority. We ate everything with great gusto. Nothing was spared save several resident mice and one large can of Mr. Bobs Baked Beans. The next order of business was a dip in the hot springs located near the cabin. The heat of the water and the massaging effect of the bubbles were pure bliss. They were putting us to sleep so we took a quick plunge in the frigid White Chuck River and headed for our bags. Pleasantly fatigued, we looked at each other with sly grins. Nothing was said, but we both knew there was one thing remaining to do.

Mr. Bob makes some mighty fine baked beans.

This Article originally appeared in the December, 1975, edition of *Signpost Magazine* entitled "Doing the Black Mountain High Route With My Good Friend Bill."

Wanderer's Wayside

AN ARGUMENT FLARES. A GUN IS BRANDISHED. Shots are fired. A man falls to the ground in the rough-and-tumble town of Darrington, Washington. The owner of the gun, a trapper named Kennedy, gets squirrelly and bolts into the mountains. Which way to go?

Head east up the Sauk River and then its tributary, the White Chuck. Keep going along a rough path until the terrain becomes too vertical, and there it is, a little burble of a hot spring deep in the Cascade Mountains. Lay low until the smoke clears and maybe memories downstream will be short and merciful.

Such was justice in 1920.

No one but the hardiest can escape upriver in that direction these days. A major rainstorm and flood in the fall of 2003 flattened the landscape and eradicated any indication of the humans who had lingered there. Gone is the hand-hewn cabin. Gone are the trails and campsites. There is no sign of the springs, the bridges, corral or shelters. What used to be one of the most popular back country areas in the region—Kennedy Hot Springs, named for that errant trapper—has been inundated with mud, woody debris and a ragged mess of rock and exposed gravel.

The area lies at 3,200 feet below the west face of Glacier Peak in the North Central Cascades. The White Chuck River cuts a path through the terrain and is joined by Kennedy Creek in what is now a jumbled flood plain. U.S. Forest Service logs note that in the early days, the hot springs trickled out as nothing more than an overheated mud hole. Over the years, it was fashioned into a 5-foot-deep enclosure capable of soaking half a dozen or so people at a time.

In their book, *Routes and Rocks*, D.F. Crowder and Rowland Tabor say the exact origin of the hot springs is unknown, but likely is a remnant of the "furnace" that fired up Glacier Peak. Deer, band-tailed pigeons and mountain goats also used the mineral-rich area as a source of salt and other nutrients.

The Sauk Indians probably found their way into the area early on, even though petroglyphs etched on now-buried rocks were never substantiated as legitimate. Possibly the Sauk leader Yowhbid traveled though Kennedy on his way to White Pass to the south. Stories told by Sauk tribal members speak of Yowhbid's prowess as a grizzly bear hunter in the 1800s using only a bow and arrow. His favorite hunting areas were the meadow systems near the headwaters of the White Chuck River.

What is known for sure is that Harry Grey blazed a route into the area in 1915 while leading a crew of 60 men to fight a wild fire on Fire Mountain. That only eight of the 60 men made it to the fire is testimonial to the ruggedness of the area. Later, Harry continued to trap along the White Chuck River all the way to the hot springs and established the first trail into the area. He then built a cabin in 1925 with the help of a Forest Service trail crew.

The next year, the cabin was made an official Forest Service guard station and sheltered a long succession of fire guards, wilderness rangers, trail crews, researchers, search-and-rescue teams and the occasional illegal squatter. For seven decades, back-country wanderers of every ilk found their way into Kennedy.

Edith Bedal, a Sauk Indian, packed in a group of mountaineers and climbed with them to the summit of Glacier Peak in 1929. Her name was one of the first signatures on the newly minted cabin, showing a date of Sept. 16, 1927. This is what Edith and her sister Jean said about their first trip into the area: "I am going back again because, for me, there is a strange and mystic charm about the place. It must be the clean beauty of the little cabin. It must be the lure of the swamp and rushing blue and milky water. It must be the mystery of the hot springs and the trail leading to Lake Byrne, beckoning up to a higher forest mecca."

Hugh Miller came to Darrington in 1913 and eventually went to work for the Forest Service. He managed the monumental construction of a 60-mile loop trail up the North Fork of the Sauk River to White Pass then back down the White Chuck, past Kennedy and back to the Sauk. Along the way, he and his crew put up a shelter every eight miles.

Many years later, a lovely woman showed up claiming she was Mrs. Hugh Miller, come to reunite with her missing husband. He had fled to the wilderness without her knowledge to manage his drinking problem. Later on, he wintered over at Kennedy Hot Springs, where he lived at the cabin and trapped martens, all to make his wife a fur cape.

Over the years, thousands of other soul-searchers, hikers and horsemen have found their way to or through Kennedy Hot Springs. The long drive up the White Chuck River led to a trailhead that opened the door to a deep-forest hiking experience second to none. This five-mile walk was, for many, their first overnight trip or day hike in true wilderness. The annual number of trekkers remained modest for a long time, with a reported 14 visitors in 1955. Kennedy back country guard Davey "Buckshot" Tucker spent part of his childhood living with his mother and brothers on Mount Three Fingers, where she was a fire lookout. In the 1950s, he and his wife, Kitty, honeymooned at Kennedy.

By 1960, 200 or more adventurers were coming, and in the 1970s the totals peaked at more than 3,000 people per season. Large groups like the Seattle Mountaineers, Mazamas and the Sierra Club were among them. Outward Bound and the National Outdoor Leadership Conference made it their first stop at the beginning of extended wilderness trips in the area. Many a wide-eyed 16-year-old from Kansas ended up peering into the darkness for bear eyes while applying Band-Aids to newly blistered feet. Probably most of the Boy Scouts in the region made it into Kennedy at one time or another.

For others, Kennedy was a pass-through to the climbing routes and remote trails of the Glacier Peak Wilderness. Access to the Pacific Crest Trail, which bisects the west flanks of Glacier Peak, was up the White Chuck past Kennedy. The June 1971 issue of National Geographic prominently featured the region in a piece called "Mexico to Canada on the Pacific Crest Trail."

The one-room log guard station was home base for hundreds of back country workers over time. The 18-by-22-foot Pacific silver fir cabin featured a large red cedar door and simple cedar furniture including a bed, table and chair. Paned-glass windows on three sides let in filtered light that highlighted a mishmash of stored tools, emergency gear, hiking equipment and the quirky artifacts of an era of use. Outside was a storage shed, rustic fresh-water spring and a one-seater outhouse down the way.

Nels Skaar and Clint Tollenaar, Scandinavian pioneers in the Darrington area, made the main kitchen cabinet, which stood in a dark corner above the sink. Thousands of hands had touched the door over the years, most of them rough, working hands looking for a bowl or a cup. Each hand left a print, the prints laid one upon the next until a sheen of sweat, soot and soil polished the doors and preserved the branded-in names of the builders.

Rangers assigned to the cabin would sit at the shaky table by the window peering out over the White Chuck River. Once the sun dropped, the cabin would darken and the only light would come from candles or an old lantern. It was often in the altered evening light that the rangers would eventually notice the penciled signatures along the bottom side of one of the wall logs. Here was where each succeeding ranger would lay claim to a piece of Kennedy history. Only those who stayed a long time signed and dated the log, extending the human history of the place.

A pot-bellied stove held center stage and served to heat the dank cabin on cold and wet days. No one stayed there who didn't come away with memories of being lulled to sleep by the nearby river, or being awakened by the army of mice that owned the cabin much of the year. A family of martens wintered over in the attic of the unoccupied cabin and worked hard at mouse control. In the summer of 1975, the ranger killed 275 mice in the line of duty and passed them on to the martens camped out under a nearby log.

In July of 1976 a major rain and flood led to a burst-out flood off the Scimitar Glacier four miles upstream. The ensuing onslaught blew through Kennedy for 12 hours and stranded 19 hikers who thought they were spending a quiet night near a pleasant back country camp. A ranger arrived the next day not knowing the plight of the hikers, but found them safe and joined them until the flooding subsided. Rangers dropped a tree across Kennedy Creek so search-and-rescue people could walk the hikers out along the washed-out White Chuck Trail to safety. It was a harbinger of things to come in 2003.

As the summer hiking season begins, miles of forest trail in the region remain inaccessible from the heavy damage of the 2003 on-slaught and a new spate of violent storms this past November. The new storms added $2.8 million to the original estimate of $10 million in damage to roads, bridges and trails. In 2003, more than 15 popular trails were destroyed, along with 20 bridges and 30 miles of the Pacific Crest scenic trail. The recent toll included the loss of nearly all bridges in the Glacier Peak Wilderness.

Because it takes three to five years for funding to catch up to the repairs needed, it's not likely the average hiker will be able to easily visit the west slopes of the Cascades anytime soon.

To get to Kennedy now, the intrepid have to start walking nine miles down the road just to get to the old trailhead at Owl Creek, skirting around blowouts and slides along the way. Then you're left to scramble over rugged terrain along the previous trail corridor. It likely replicates much of what Harry Grey found nearly a century ago when he worked his way up the valley. Another option is to hike the sketchy Lost Creek Ridge Trail for 11 miles to Lake Byrne, then drop down the 90 switchbacks to the Kennedy Basin. Unfortunately, there is no verified way across the White Chuck River, so the territory from that angle remains virtually inaccessible.

So, what to do?

Some would leave well enough alone and not rebuild access to the area, thereby honoring the intent of the Wilderness Act of 1964. Significant language in the law defines "wilderness" as lands that generally appear "to have been affected primarily by the forces of nature" and offer "outstanding opportunities for solitude or a primitive and unconfined type of recreation."

From that perspective, the floods of 2003 and 2006 along the western slopes of the Cascades maintain the intended integrity of the Wilderness Act in its strictest sense, letting nature take its course. But what of the realities of human nature, and our urge to explore and develop? What obligation does the Forest Service have to put things back the way they were, especially with such tightly restricted funding?

As of now, a new trail has been surveyed into the Kennedy area, but construction timelines remain unclear. The new trail would be carved high above the mercurial White Chuck River in hopes of avoiding the unstable nature of the river bottom. Should nothing be done, the area could be left open for a new generation of cross-country hikers to explore. Others might retrace their steps in the valley to recall the way it was.

Old man Kennedy had his own worries 77 years earlier. His conscience ate at him until he decided to march out to Darrington and give himself up. The man he'd shot had recovered and was long gone by the time he showed up. The locals had pretty much forgotten about the incident. Kennedy, in his turn, added his story to the inventory of those who have found their way into this quiet place at the head of the valley.

This article originally appeared in the May 27th, 2007 edition of the *Seattle Times Pacific Magazine* entitled "The Wanderers Wayside."

Green Mountain sunset.

Thank You

WRITTEN EFFORTS SUCH AS THIS are refined and enriched with the help of many people. My thanks go out to my wife Jeanne, my companion in many trips beyond the end of the road and supporter of my writing. Here's to Tony Angell, advisor and mentor, Bill Hansen, reader and fellow traveler, Bernie Smith, dedicated naturalist and friend, and Katie Kurtz, who set aside familial loyalties and edited

About the Author

RUSS HANBEY is a Northwest native and writer. During his career as a classroom teacher, Russ was able to spend summers working for the Forest Service and the Student Conservation Association. He specializes in creative non-fiction, natural history and environmental education writings. He is a specialist in wilderness and remote site restoration.

Russ divides his time between Tucson, Arizona and Seattle, Washington.

Please visit his website, *russhanbey.com*, for further information.

Author and wife, Jeanne, high atop Mt. Pugh with Glacier Peak in back ground, North Central Cascades. August, 1979. Photo by Wayne Katon

CPSIA information can be obtained
at www.ICGtesting.com
Printed in the USA
FSHW021500281118
54095FS